Roommates from Beyond

How to Live in a Haunted Home

Roommates from Beyond

How to Live in a Haunted Home

Tonya & Joey Madia

New Mystics Enterprises, Inc.

Leavittsburg, Ohio

Roommates from Beyond:
How to Live in a Haunted Home

Copyright Tonya and Joey Madia, 2020

All rights reserved.
No part of this book may be used or reproduced
without permission from the publisher.

Front and back cover by Chuck Regan

ISBN: 978-0-9821842-3-3

New Mystics Enterprises, Inc.
Leavittsburg, Ohio
www.newmystics.com

Acknowledgments

Endless gratitude and thanks:

To all of our mentors, living and dead, whose professionalism, passion, patience, and guidance are always present in the high-quality work we endeavor to do.

To the Mothman Irregulars for the joy of countless hours in the field learning and practicing our craft and deep conversations over meals at Harris' Steakhouse (aka the Mothman Diner) in Point Pleasant, West Virginia and for being our teachers, colleagues, and friends.

To the RTC: You know who you are and how valuable your insights will be to the world.

To the many radio and podcast hosts and event and festival organizers who have invited us to share our experiences, theories, and ways of working with your audiences.

To the producers at Sky Door Network, KGRA Radio, and ERRT Radio for giving us a weekly platform to share our experiences and those of our guests.

To our growing list of clients who trust us to come into their homes and businesses, interact with their families, and tell their stories.

To Emily Mittermaier, fellow investigator and business partner, for the Foreword and the friendship.

And, most especially,

To the ghosts and spirits in the Webb Memorial Library in Morehead City, North Carolina and elsewhere that have taught us so much about the nature of Reality, Life after Death, and Parallel Dimensions.

Dedication

To our mentor, publisher, and friend, Rosemary Ellen Guiley, who teaches us in death as she did for a decade in life.

Table of Contents

Acknowledgments v
Dedication vii
Foreword xiii
Introduction 1
    Who We Are 1
    Tonya Madia, RYT, RMT, LMT 1
    A Little Bit about Tonya's Family History 2
    Joey Madia 8
    A Little Bit about Joey's Family History 8
    Our Investigative Background 10
    Why We Wrote This Book 11
    Why Would I Live in a Haunted Home or Work in a Haunted Space? 12
    What We Hope You'll Gain from Reading (and Using!) This Book 13
Important Terminology 17
    Spirits and Ghosts 17
    Light Entities/Celestial Beings 18
    Dark Entities 18
    Stages of Hauntings 19
    Cynics, Skeptics, and Over-Enthusiasts 21
Our 10-Point Philosophy (A Paranormal Bill of Rights) 25
A Few Words Concerning Intention 27
The Tools of Our Trade 29
    Your Body, Senses, and Consciousness are the Best Equipment 29
    Other Equipment 30

Cultivate Strong Research Skills 31
Cultivate the Art and Craft of Interviewing 32
A Basic Knowledge of Character and Narrative Structure is Essential 34
Knowing the Value and Limitations of Synchronicity 35
Transdisciplinarity and the Quest for Parallels and Patterns .. 36

Part I: Our Haunted Homes 41
Mesa, Arizona (Tonya's story) 43
Brick Township, New Jersey 45
Tinton Falls, New Jersey 49
Fairmont, West Virginia (aka "The Holler") 59
Beaufort, North Carolina 71
Leavittsburg, Ohio 85
Nonhuman Entities 91
The "Mothman Effect" 93
Closing a Portal with Spiritual and Celestial Guidance 96
An Unexpected Family Visitor 98

Part II: From Our Case Files 101
Introduction 103
A Tragic Case of Misidentification in Ohio 105
A Dangerous Case in Pennsylvania 113
The Initial Interview 113
A Not So Subtle Warning to Keep Away 114
The Video Interview and a Surprising Revelation 115
Invaluable Guidance from Beyond 117
The Site Visit 118
Generations of Hauntings in a Multi-Family Victorian 123
Taking the Case History during Our Initial Visit 123

Our Return Visit 127

All in the Family 129

A Basement and Bedroom Intruder 135

Helping a Friend with a Follow-Home 139

Buyer Beware 143

Part III: More from Our Case Files: Haunted Buildings/Places of Business 147

Our Old Friend, the Webb, Morehead City, North Carolina 149

A Very Haunted Historical Society Museum 155

Hurt Feelings in a Family Cemetery 161

Discovery of a Murder at a Drive-In 165

Part IV: Practical Matters: What to Do When Your Home Is Being Haunted 167

Catch the Haunting Early 169

    Eliminate Mundane Causes for Phenomena 169

    Use Your Intuition 169

    Pay Attention to the Behavior of Pets and Children 170

    Getting Outside Help 172

    Revisiting the Four Stages of a Haunting 172

What's the Story? 175

    A Case Study Applying the Three 3s 177

Strategies for Managing or Ending a Haunting 179

    Respect 179

    Intention 179

    Protecting, Clearing, and Warding Your Home 180

The Role of Consciousness 189

Communication 191

Setting Boundaries and Negotiation 195

Ending a Haunting in Your Home 199

Closing Thoughts 203
Bibliography.. 205
Our Paranormal Bill of Rights 207
Other Books by Tonya and Joey Madia...................... 211
Outer Realms Bath Works 213

Foreword

By Emily Mittermaier

The beauty of the paranormal is that none of us have all of the answers. While we may have our theories on what a ghost is or have experiences that lead us to accept certain ideas about why entities haunt our homes, no one has undeniable proof of what hauntings are and why they occur.

You may be asking yourself why, if no one has definitive answers about hauntings, should you read a book about what hauntings are and how to deal with them? The answer is simple—because we cannot further our understanding of the paranormal without learning from others' experiences and research.

If you are living with an otherworldly roommate, chances are you are afraid—either of whatever is residing in your home or of how people will react when you tell them you have a ghost in your house. Maybe even both! In *Roommates from Beyond,* Tonya and Joey Madia are your seasoned guides who will help you understand common types of hauntings and phenomena, demystify and possibly debunk strange activity you may be experiencing, and empower you to manage the phenomena manifesting in your home, all based on their years of experiencing, researching, and investigating the paranormal.

Reading Tonya and Joey's personal experiences detailed in this book was like a trip down memory lane for me. Many of the stories I've heard over the course of our many years together as friends and colleagues. Some of the experiences I was even there to witness firsthand! We've spent countless hours wandering around in the darkness of night searching for ghosts and cryptids in the hills of West Virginia, listening for disembodied voices and flickers of apparitions in our respective homes, and comparing research on all manner of topics ranging from ghosts and the Mothman to conspiracy theories and time travel.

Reading through the case files of clients who sought help and answers from Tonya and Joey reiterated the importance of thorough research, logic, and compassion when helping others understand what is happening in their home.

Reading the guidance and advice for how to handle a haunting in your home reinforced what I consider to be something paramount to the study of the paranormal—respect. We don't know who or what is haunting our homes, nor should we presume to. Keeping an open mind, doing your due diligence, and treating the unknown with respect is key to understanding and appreciating the paranormal.

We may never have all the answers, but *Roommates from Beyond* is a key piece in figuring out the paranormal puzzle.

Emily Mittermaier is a paranormal investigator, sensitive, and photographer. She is the co-owner of Outer Realms Bathworks (outerrealmsbathworks.com). She travels extensively and documents her experiences on her blog, A Traveling Spirit (atravelingspirit.com). You can also follow her on Facebook and Instagram.

Introduction

Welcome to our carefully designed handbook for hauntings!

There are so many tools we want to share, guidance and recommendations we want to give and make, and stories and cases to present, that we promise to keep this introduction brief. But, before we get into the practical, tried and true advice for managing hauntings in your home (or business)—based on our lifetime as experiencers and over a decade as professional paranormal researchers, lecturers, and investigators—we want to cover the basics of the Who, Why, and What of this book.

Who We Are

Although author biographies traditionally appear in the back of the book (and this one is no exception), we also wanted to each take a moment to introduce ourselves to you at the onset. Additionally, we also share a little of our family histories. Researchers identified a long time ago that experiencers often have a family history of paranormal encounters.

This is certainly the case for us.

Tonya Madia, RYT, RMT, LMT

From the time I was very young, I was told that I had a vivid imagination. This observation about me was accurate but also overused. I knew that the disembodied footsteps, voices, and sensations of being watched were not just my imagination, as I was so often told. I was very fortunate to have a grandmother and many other mentors throughout my life who would gently guide me onto the path that would eventually allow me to tap fully into my own natural intuitive abilities.

Today I am a Certified Hypnotist, Reiki Master, medium, yoga teacher, and massage therapist in part because of the teachings and assistance I received from those mentors, and it is because of their guidance that I am passionate about helping others. My lifelong experiences with the paranormal and encounters as a medium have led me to state with surety that consciousness can survive the death of the physical body. I love being asked to do readings, mentor other mediums, and investigate active locations. I feel extremely blessed to have the opportunity to help so many others on their life's journey. My first book, *Living the Intuitive Life: Cultivating Extraordinary Awareness*, is a guidebook for anyone interested in developing their own natural intuitive abilities. My second book, *Watch out for the Hallway: Our Two-Year Investigation of the Most Haunted Library in North Carolina*, coauthored with Joey, illustrates how important it is to trust your experiences and not dismiss them as imagination.

I love being the cohost of our weekly show, *Into the Outer Realms* and talking with other hosts on radio and podcasts. I also enjoy traveling and presenting at paranormal events and conventions with Joey, as well as attending paranormal events as a vendor with Emily Mittermaier, my business partner and cofounder of Outer Realms Bath Works, a business dedicated to creating high-quality paranormal-themed candles, soaps, and bath works and creepy dolls.

A Little Bit about Tonya's Family History

My paternal grandmother Clara was a psychic medium like I am, although, unlike me, it was her early childhood experiences that led her to delve into the realm of the paranormal. My own explorations came much later in life, when I began studying the healing arts and working with energy. Clara's mother, my great grandmother Osa, had experiences at a young age and they both shared tales of classic haunting phenomena.

My grandmother became so interested in the paranormal that she filled numerous notebooks with details about her research and experiences. I have been the custodian of these notebooks since my grandmother's passing in 1990, and I am working on transcribing them as part of a book I am writing about Clara and her fascinating life. These notebooks contain hundreds of pages of notes, research, automatic writing, astral travel experiences, and spirit board transcripts, and once transcribed and narrated, will provide a wealth of information about communication with the Other Side.

In one of her many notebooks, Clara wrote of the following experiences:

Many times after my grandmother passed on I heard my name called in a voice that seemed to be hers. I would wake from sleep to full consciousness with the sound of my name ringing in my head, or I'd hear her call me from another room and go to see if someone were there, or had spoken. Those around me laughed and said it was just my imagination. But I knew I had heard her call. I wondered why, and wished that I were not frightened each time; then perhaps she could let me know what it was she wanted.

This account reminded me very much of my earliest paranormal experience, which I recount in detail in our book *Watch out for the Hallway.*

My grandmother goes on to share her experiences from the other side after the loss of my paternal grandfather, Vivian:

Years ago, when my husband was killed in an automobile train accident [his car stalled on the train tracks and he was struck and killed by an oncoming train] I was overcome with the loss and would not face the fact that he was gone. I was in Florida shortly after his death, and grieving for him with every thought. I could not eat or sleep or cease my weeping. Then one night as I lay in the dark, so lonely and despondent, I heard his voice call my name. Once I listened with all my being, he called again softly. I sat up and at the foot of my bed saw him standing there, as whole and healthy as he had ever been. He smiled and said 'don't cry honey see I'm fine,' and then he was gone. I cried out after him to stay, and I began to weep again. Then all at once, I felt warm and at peace and ceased my crying. I felt his presence beside me, and I slept peacefully for the first time since his death.

I was especially excited to discover this entry in the notebook, as I have a very vivid memory of my grandmother relaying this account to me when I was seven years old.

In another entry, my grandmother writes about a UFO sighting she had in 1973:

Well my experiences are varied to say the least. Saturday evening when we took Helen [a close friend and fellow researcher] home from a visit here, I happened to look up, for I felt compelled to do so, and there above us darting in and out of the clouds were three bright objects. I called attention to them and Helen and I were watching them dart about the heavens as if in a game of chase. Mama was sitting in the car and called out, "what are you all looking at?" I said, "we are watching these UFOs." She then joined us and after a while she spotted them also. They looked like large bright stars. They were above the clouds for every once in a while they disappeared into them. Then they would dart out across the sky or straight down, growing brighter as they fell. I wish I had had binoculars along for they were not visible when we arrived home. The next day on the news they reported that UFOs had been spotted over Georgia. We didn't report them but they were also spotted over Van Buren Arkansas.

Doing some research into the Georgia sighting, I was able to find the following reports of UFO sightings in the state:
- August 31, 1973: Several police officers in Cordele, Georgia reported seeing large bright objects moving through the sky, just below the stars.
- September 1973: A farmer near Macon, Georgia fired several shots at a large, bright, flying object as it drifted toward his house and vanished into the ground.
- October 1973: In Fitzgerald, Georgia, southeast of Cordele, there were reports of a strange light, larger than a star, moving around in the sky.

I found all of these accounts in digital news articles, which you can find by doing an Internet search using: "Georgia UFO sightings 1973." Also, in a wonderful case of synchronicity, on the day before this book was scheduled to go to the printer, Joey found them referenced in a May 1974 article by John Keel in *Saga* magazine.

Because Clara dated her entry about the sighting with only the year, and not the month and day, it is impossible to know whether one of these is the same Georgia sighting she refers to in her notebook. However, these sightings are certainly interesting in that they took place in the same year and approximately 800 miles southeast of the location of her sighting.

Another entry from the same notebook describes what seems to be a bout of sleep paralysis that took place in 1974:

Saturday night as I was practicing relaxation and astral projection techniques I began to feel myself drift, then I clearly heard a voice call my name, then, the words "Tell my wife." I asked who it was and what I should tell, but only got an impression, perhaps it was "Dr. Patton." I then I became fully conscious, however soon I was drifting once more. When I later woke, I found I had lain from somewhere around 12:15 AM when I first woke, until 5 AM in the relaxed position on my back. It was all I could do to make myself move at all. I had a very heavy pressure and a sick feeling in my solar plexus. My heart pounded heavily and I felt very uncomfortable. It was quite some time before I began to feel normal again. I do not like this sort of thing but I must continue in my search.

This entry was of particular interest to me because of my own experiences with sleep paralysis, which took place from the time I was a teenager and well into my adulthood. I write about many of these experiences in the section about our experiences living in haunted homes.

Clara also transcribed several spirit board sessions. I chose to share the one below because it seems to shed some light on the way in which spirits can communicate to the living:

July, 1970:
Question: Why can't we talk to just anyone we want to and why can't you always come through to us?
Answer: I must find channel.

Question: How do you come through and why do you hesitate sometimes?
Answer: Like computer, must search memory some.
Question: Do most spirits have to use guides to reach us?
Answer: Usually, some make direct perception.
Question: Why did you come through for us?
Answer: Don't know I just saw you. You sometimes believe we can do miraculous [sic] but we are limited to much the same things you are. Sometimes we are not allowed to do the things you ask and sometimes we are required to provide information that will cause you to think about these matters.

(The next section of the transcript from this session sheds light on an encounter that Clara's brother, my great uncle, had with a negative entity.)

Question: When Jimmy saw the ugly face float at him who was it?
Answer: That was an evil one.
Question: Could this happen to us?
Answer: We will protect you.
Question: Why did he scare Jimmy like that?
Answer: He considered Jim an intruder.

In addition to my grandmother and great grandmother's experiences, my mother had several encounters with the paranormal, especially as a young child. Just one year before her passing, my mother pressed me to write down the experiences that had affected her most. I was glad she did.

Rocks on the Porch: Van Buren, Arkansas, 1953

When my mother was six years old, her stepfather rented an old house for the family in Crawford County. It was a one-story log house, with a wood stove, and a large porch. The house was in the country and was surrounded by a barbed-wire fence. Every night, just after sunset, rocks would start hitting the porch. Everyone in the family could see the rocks coming up on the porch but they could not determine where the rocks were coming from. They appeared from thin air and then hurled themselves, full speed, onto the porch. The *next morning the porch would be covered in rocks. They were never able to determine where the rocks came from.*

As the rocks were hitting the porch, a white horse would be seen running through the yard. It would run right through the barbed-wire fence and then disappear. Once the horse disappeared, the rocks would stop. This would happen at the same time every evening, and eventually they found another rental home and moved away.

Rocks hurled at the house is classic poltergeist activity; however, the phantom horse and the fact that this type of activity ceased once they moved from the house, lead me to think that the activity was tied to the house. The fact that the activity occurred at the same time every evening points to the phenomenon being the result of a residual haunting. Because my mother was always a sensitive with psychic abilities of her own, it is possible that her presence in the home acted as a battery, charging the environment and elevating the intensity of the haunting.

My mother also had some experiences with deceased loved ones.

The first was when she was seven years old. At her grandfather's viewing, my mother's stepmother made her kiss her grandfather goodbye. As she walked away she was crying and very clearly heard him say, "Sue honey, don't worry… it's okay." She turned and went back to the casket because she was convinced that he was still alive.

This account reminds me of Clara's childhood experience of hearing her grandmother, and my experience of hearing my name called when I was five years old. Children are much more open to hearing and communicating with the spirit realm because they have not yet been conditioned to believe that they cannot.

My mother had another encounter years later, when my paternal grandfather who died one day before my mother was born came to visit.

This took place in 1969. My father was sleeping and my mother was lying awake in bed. As she lay there, she looked over at the door and saw the apparition of a man. She immediately recognized him from photographs as my dad's father, Vivian. She watched him go into my bedroom and after a few moments, he came out of my room and went into my brother's room. My mother always felt that he was coming to see his grandchildren.

I think it is very interesting to note that, from a very young age, I felt a strong connection to Vivian, my paternal grandfather. I remember feeling as if I knew him when I would look at photos of him, although of course I never met him. Or did I? Similarly, our daughter Jolie always had a strong interest and connection to my grandmother Clara, who died nine years before Jolie was born, and to Vivian as well. From a very young age, Jolie would often fascinate me by sharing facts about her great-grandmother that she should not have known.

Very much in keeping with family tradition, Jolie is a talented psychic medium who has assisted us on cases, especially during the two years at the Webb Memorial Library.

Joey Madia

Since I was a boy, reading Hardy Boys and other adventures in my bed every Saturday morning, I have been fascinated with Story. So much so that I spent more time in the Performing Arts wing of my middle and high schools than I did at home and I double majored in Theatre and English Literature in college. Since my graduation in 1990, I have been a professional storyteller and teacher. When I am not investigating, teaching, or writing about strange phenomena, I am a novelist, actor, director, playwright, screenwriter, Escape Room designer, and podcast and YouTube host. For twenty-two years, I have specialized in bringing true stories to the stage, page, and screen, including people's journeys through drug and alcohol addiction, teen pregnancy, mental illness, violence, HIV and AIDS, and, of course, the paranormal. My screenplay *The Man at the Foot of the Bed* (a paranormal thriller based on a true story) has been a two-time Official Selection and a Beverly Hills Film Festival invitee. My novel series, The Stanton Chronicles, combines history, mystery, and the paranormal. Most importantly, where all of my life experiences professionally and personally come together is in applying the skills of a story analyst and training in a variety of spiritual systems to our paranormal investigations.

A Little Bit about Joey's Family History

It was not until nine months before the publication of this book, after a colleague suggested that I explore my ancestry to find those who engaged in spiritual and occult practices—because she was certain that there were those who had—that I took out the family tree I had been carrying around since an elementary school assignment four decades ago and began to do some research into my great-grandparents.

Having grown up with "proud-to-be-American" first- and second-generation Italian immigrant grandparents on both sides, a pride that was instilled in my mother and especially my father, a veteran of the Vietnam War, I knew well enough that, outside of our being Roman Catholic—one of the most mystical of religions, even though most Catholics do not see it that way—there was not much interest in the paranormal and supernatural and, in general, neither side of the family was much inclined to talk about the past and our ancestors' lives in Sicily, Calabria, and Naples.

The only person in my family that I knew had any interest or experience with spirituality and the paranormal was my Aunt Annette, my father's sister. From the time I was little she would tell me stories that were really lessons about connecting with a higher source and living a deeply spiritual life. Although she was beloved by everyone in the family, she was also known as "odd Aunt Annette," who studied herbology and acupressure and went to a lot of Native American pow-wows, strange workshops, and exotic places all around the world.

After Tonya and I moved to New Jersey in our late twenties, we began to have weekly dinners with Aunt Annette and her husband, who was also a spiritual seeker and healer, and from there we began to study with them various spiritual systems. They introduced us to shamanism, meditation, and lucid dreaming. It was Aunt Annette who saw in Tonya her potential as an energy healer.

After Aunt Annette passed away suddenly about fifteen years ago, I did not give much thought to my family connections to the esoteric and occult. Aunt Annette had never spoken anything about it. But when our colleague suggested I look into it, I took two steps right away. First, I began studying the Italian form of wicca or paganism known as *stregheria*. At the same time, I began asking Aunt Annette's sister, who is a spiritually adept sensitive and Reiki Master, about our family history.

The two sides of my family are very close. My paternal grandfather was my maternal uncle's Confirmation godfather and one of my maternal great-grandmothers, who was very close friends with one of my paternal great-grandmothers, was the one who brought my parents together, for which I am very grateful.

As it turns out, three of my four great-grandmothers were known for or practiced some form of spirituality and occultism outside of the boundaries of the Catholic Church. The great-grandmother who got my parents together, who came from Sicily, was referred to as a "mistress of the occult." I received this information from a second cousin when I mentioned my genealogical research on an episode of our weekly livestream, *Into the Outer Realms*. Her name was Palma, most likely named in honor of Palm Sunday. Since we began discussing her on the show, she has been visiting us here at our home.

One of my paternal great-grandmothers, Maria Carolina (my sister is named Carolyn Marie for her), received information in dreams, was considered "very tuned in" in the neighborhood, and she learned her skills from her mother, Lucia.

As I mentioned, Palma's very close friend was my other paternal great-grandmother, Antoinette, who also had a reputation for being a psychic.

No wonder, with at least four generations of sensitives and psychics on both sides of her family line, that our daughter, Jolie, is such a skilled psychic medium.

Our Investigative Background

As many of the readers of this book already know, our lives changed in profound ways in August 2009 when we experienced an interdimensional being emerging into and out of a portal in Point Pleasant, West Virginia. Missing time and space–time disruption were a key part of that experience and it was at that point that Joey decided that, if the paranormal was going to keep studying us, we were going to study it back.

For the next ten years we studied under the tutelage of well-known author, radio and TV personality, and investigator Rosemary Ellen Guiley. Although we have developed our own unique philosophy and investigative style because of our being married and having different as well as overlapping skill sets, we owe all that we have done in the realm of the paranormal to Rosemary's teaching, guidance, and friendship.

In 2016, we had the opportunity to investigate a haunted library in North Carolina. That investigation lasted two years, comprising 75 nights and 150 hours and involving over 500 guest investigators, many of whom were sensitives, psychics, and/or mediums. We cannot express how much we learned during that investigation on proper techniques, how to build a respectful/equitable relationship with ghosts and spirits, how to deal safely and effectively with dark entities, and how ghosts and spirits—and the places that they haunt—can change over time.

Since 2017, we have been honored to undertake many investigations in homes and work spaces, some of which we discuss in this book.

All of these experiences have contributed to our philosophy and how we use the tools of the paranormal investigator.

Why We Wrote This Book

With all of the books that have been written on the subject of haunted houses, you may be asking, "Why is this one different?" Great question! We asked ourselves the same question many times prior to our decision to sit down and actually write this book.

There are several answers. First, we purposely chose the word "home" instead of "house" because this is not a book that stops at the reporting of various cases of hauntings. The term *haunted house* has come to mean something akin to a paid Halloween thrill-ride or horror film scenario. It is a place you want to leave or perhaps destroy. We offer solutions outside of abandonment, banishment, and exorcism. The personal stories of our homes and details of our cases are the practical portion of the book that helps us to illustrate how the tools and practices we use actually work in real-life situations. The true value of this book is in helping people find their way to solutions. Packing up and leaving is rarely an option, nor is it something people want to do. Our homes are important to us. Part of the reason hauntings are difficult is because they are, on varying levels, an invasion. You have an unwanted guest—which does not mean a demon or even a dangerous ghost or spirit. Just like a cousin who comes for the weekend and stays a month, or a drunken uncle shouting about politics at Thanksgiving and criticizing how you cooked the turkey, it is more about the inconvenience of having your space invaded. Of having things moved. Of being woken up in the middle of the night because doors are slamming and lights are flickering or there are footsteps on the stairs.

Based on our own considerable experience of twenty-five years of living in haunted homes and numerous cases where we have helped others with theirs, we want this book to be more than something you read out of curiosity, or passing interest, or even to get a good scare before bed. We want it to be a handbook you use to navigate successfully a situation where someone or something is haunting your home.

Why Would I Live in a Haunted Home or Work in a Haunted Space?

We understand why some of you might ask. All we can say is, we have encountered all kinds of ghosts and spirits throughout our lives and especially over the last two decades, and, in all honesty, many of them are pleasant—even funny—and have something profound to teach us. We see our work with the entities we encounter to be very much a two-way street. We have received an abundance of gifts from the ghosts and spirits we have shared various spaces with over the years.

We mentioned funny. While we were presenting at a conference a few years ago, a woman approached Tonya and asked if there was someone around her. Tonya was instantly able to see who it was. It was the woman's father—and he appeared as an Elvis impersonator! The woman shared that that was indeed the sense of humor her father had in life! That same day, there was also a rugged mountaineer with fur cap, backpack, and walking stick near one of Tonya's colleagues (who works for a college that has a mountaineer for a mascot). We have also had ghosts with a quick wit and sharp senses of humor come through spirit boxes and other communication devices with funny and even at times sarcastic questions and responses.

In all fairness to both you and to the ghosts or spirits you might encounter, we also have a question for you: What is your threshold for this kind of thing?

Over time, as we have experienced both the Light and Dark sides of the paranormal on a weekly and sometimes daily basis, our own answer to this question has continually changed. Yours no doubt will as well. There is sometimes a fine line between an interesting or funny haunting that you welcome as a value-added part of your life and something that becomes oppressive or intrusive.

The litmus test for this question is how safe you feel in your home, because safety and security are your right. Even the friendliest ghost can at times behave like an intruder. When they appear in your bedroom or outside the curtain while you are taking a shower—as the ghosts of two military men did to our teenage daughter—you are having your boundaries overstepped and you have every right to express that. You might not want things moved, or hidden, or to have a spirit or ghost jump out at you when you are not expecting it.

When the time comes to ask them to respect boundaries or even leave your space, the practical sections of this handbook will help.

A word of advice about what you might be getting yourself into when it comes to living in a home with haunting activity: Some houses resist you moving in. Everything seems to go wrong—movers don't show up, all kinds of delays are experienced, and miscommunication seems to be a daily occurrence.

Other houses, on the other hand, won't let you go.

As you will read in the sections to come, we have experienced both.

So choose your homes with care.

What We Hope You'll Gain from Reading (and Using!) This Book

There is a lot of good news these days in the field of paranormal research. More people than ever before (including many leading scientists) believe that consciousness survives death and that spirits and ghosts are real. Additionally, more people than ever before are openly admitting that they have had these experiences. The bad news is that there is a lot of distorted or just plain wrong information out there, coming from a variety of sources. Given the growing acceptance of and interest in the paranormal, some producers and hosts of TV "reality" shows and YouTube channels and authors of independently published, inadequately researched books are taking advantage of the opportunity to engage with a field about which they understand little to increase their ratings, views, and sales.

Even worse, they are preying on people's fears, assuming everything is (or portraying everything as) a demon or evil, and exploiting people's experiences instead of helping them and using the gathered data as a teaching tool.

Because we are seeing considerable evidence that the prevalence of hauntings in homes and elsewhere is increasing in frequency and duration and people are unsure where to turn for help, we decided to write this book.

By the time you are finished reading *Roommates from Beyond*, we want you to have the knowledge, tools, and confidence needed to manage a haunting in your home. We want to teach you how to protect yourself, gather necessary information about who or what is haunting your home (and why!), and how to proceed based on the data you collect.

Not all haunting situations are safe. We chose the cases for this book in part to show the dangers you might face. But do not be afraid. You do not have to face a haunting alone. If there is evidence of a dark entity that is causing harm and refuses to leave or change its behavior, and more aggressive steps need to be taken, then you can enlist outside help—from both sides of the veil—to provide guidance on how to proceed.

We are here to help.

In many cases we are brought in on, what we see happening—which can be frustrating, counterproductive, and potentially dangerous for the living and the dead—is that assumptions are made, the homeowner overreacts and calls in either amateur investigators, exploitative ones, or someone who is all too happy to banish the source of the haunting to some dark void without taking the time to even try to understand the questions we outlined above.

This is happening all too often.

Here is a quick example (and we are grateful that the amateur investigators contacted us beforehand): A few people with some experiences with the paranormal whom we had briefly mentored while doing the two-year Webb Library investigation contacted us. They had purchased some equipment and put out the word that they were seeking places to investigate. An acquaintance sent them a video. After watching it, one of the investigators said she saw a face about a foot off the floor. The homeowner hypothesized that it was the ghost of the previous owner and that he was playing with their cat. This is an important fact to keep in mind.

The homeowner reported that she had thought the ghost had gotten into bed with her. Her housekeeper had also seen it as a full-bodied apparition at least three times. So, of course, there was disruption and cause for concern. No ghost has a right to get into bed with you without permission.

The problem with the situation was that one of the other investigators did not intend to bring any of their equipment. She did not intend to ask questions. In essence, she did not intend to be an investigator. Her sole intention was to "push [the entity] out," which put her more in the role of an ignorant would-be exorcist.

We hope you see the problems with this approach. The former homeowner has understandable attachments to the house. Importantly, the entity was harming neither the cat nor the housekeeper. In fact, it was the opposite. The report was that the ghost was *playing with* the cat. This is not always the case. Often pets are terrorized or even killed. One of the cases later in the book involves exactly that. There was also no evidence of anything else that indicated the potential for danger to any of the inhabitants.

The investigators took our advice to do a proper investigation and to communicate with the ghost. Well… that was their intention, anyway. Unfortunately, when they arrived the nervous homeowner had been drinking and they did not proceed with an investigation. They made the right decision. We have encountered this situation enough over the years to say without question that alcohol and paranormal investigations do not mix. Alcohol weakens your energetic field and leaves you vulnerable to psychic attack and attachment. In general, you should never consume alcohol before any type of energy work, spiritual practice, or paranormal investigation. Alcohol also impairs your judgment, which is another reason to avoid spirits before investigating *Spirits*.

Important Terminology

Although we cannot turn you into a seasoned professional paranormal investigator by the end of this book, we are going to teach you enough about the work that we do to understand what a haunting is and how to manage or resolve it. Defining the terminology up front also allows us to present the stories of our haunted homes and some of our cases without a lot of technical explanation cluttering up and slowing the narrative down.

Spirits and Ghosts

A *spirit* is a former human being who has crossed over to another dimension and returns now and again, often with more frequency right after death and in the few months after. They may return to give guidance or to check in with family and friends. We have been blessed over the years to have visits and receive help from several of our deceased relatives in the form of spirits. They have at times stopped by just to check in—as Joey's maternal grandfather does every three years or so—and others have been present in our home for weeks if we are having health issues or dealing with a difficult haunting.

A *ghost* is a former human being who has not yet crossed over to another dimension. A ghost remains on the Earthly plane for some specific reason. Perhaps they are getting something they need here, like an alcohol or tobacco fix from an unsuspecting living person. Perhaps the lure of "the Light" is not strong enough to outweigh their attachments to their life on Earth. Perhaps they are afraid of going into "the Light" because of something they did while they were alive or simply fear of the unknown. In some cases, the deceased do not know they are dead. We have also encountered ghosts, some of which we describe in this book, who had suffered a head trauma and were confused about where they were or where they should be. During the course of our work we have crossed over a wide variety of ghosts, each of whom met at least one of the criteria listed above. The crossing over process can vary in length and complexity and spirits and even archangels and our guides have been present to assist.

We have never forced a ghost to cross over. In some instances, a few of which you will read about in the case section of this book, they are reluctant and we will try again and call for help from a higher source. But there have been times when the ghost was not ready and, since they were doing no harm to anyone, we did not persist.

Light Entities/Celestial Beings

It was during the final edits to this book that we added this section. Without falling into the realm of religious names, definitions, and origin stories, these are nonhuman entities that have come to be understood as spirit guides, archangels, guardian angels, interstellar watchers, and other protectors and teachers of humankind. We have included this classification because we have increasingly come to seek the help of and receive guidance from these types of entities and we provide tools for calling upon and acknowledging them in your own life and when engaging with or managing hauntings in the final section of the book.

Dark Entities

For a variety of reasons, over the past several years we have adopted the term *dark entities* to describe nonhuman sentient beings that feed on human energy, primarily on our stress, anger, and fear. This heading of *dark entities* can cover a wide range of phenomena, from shadow people to djinn, from tulpas to malevolent interdimensional beings, to demons. Using this blank term takes limiting frames like religion and cultural bias out of the discussion so we can focus on the problems these beings cause without getting caught up in the nuances of names or making wrong assumptions due to a stereotype.

Stages of Hauntings

There are four stages of hauntings, each more complex and dangerous than the one that precedes it. Demonologists most often use this spectrum strictly in terms of stages of possession, but we have found it useful to apply these categorizations to all types of haunting phenomena. It is especially helpful when engaging with or attempting to manage a haunting, so you can gauge where the haunting is and what your options and next actions may be at any given stage, and we refer to them often in the pages to come.

It is important to seek help from investigators, clergy, energy healers, and other appropriate resources before things get so bad with a haunting that you are in danger or are considering leaving the home for good. The lower you go on the scale, the more common the phenomena. The experiences we have had in our various homes and during cases that we have completed as investigators fall mostly into the areas of Manifestation and Infestation, although we have had experiences with both Oppression and Possession.

We offer brief explanations here and go into more detail in the actual experiences and cases we report.

Manifestation

In a few words, *manifestation* is evidence of phenomena that creates awareness that something paranormal is in your home or professional space. This can range from poltergeist activity (from German for "noisy ghost"; this might be objects moving or going missing, doors and windows opening and closing; and other low-level phenomena) to sensing a presence, hearing footsteps, seeing shadows, smelling phantom odors, or even seeing a full-bodied apparition. Many of the homes we have lived in had manifestation of one type or another. Depending on your threshold for this kind of activity, some people do not mind a little manifestation in their home and some even welcome it.

To the last group we say, *careful what you wish for.*

Infestation

As you will read in the chapters that follow, movement from manifestation to *infestation* can be abrupt, changing the overall situation in a heartbeat. There is nothing fun about infestation. The phenomena are persistent at this level and may disrupt your peace of mind, routine, sleep habits, and cause you to feel unsafe in a place that should be your primary zone of safety. Infestation is like being the victim of a home robbery. We were unfortunate enough to experience this stage of haunting activity in a home that we rented in Tinton Falls, New Jersey—an experience we share with you in considerable detail in a later chapter. The infestation in that home was so intense that it bled over—pardon the pun—into oppression. It is imperative to seek outside guidance if the phenomena in your home has moved to infestation. Things can only get worse as the ghost or other entity becomes empowered and entrenched over time.

Oppression

At the *oppression* stage of a haunting, people are suffering. Sleep deprivation and lack of peace of mind can make them irritable. Fear and stress are incredibly debilitating over time, in addition to being a rich energy feast for the dark entities we mentioned earlier. Oppression may cause people's relationships to deteriorate, cause problems with concentration and at their job, and lead to thoughts of harming themselves or others. In a few of the cases presented in this book, you will see the results of oppression. At times oppression can take the form of physical danger. As you will read in one of the cases, a dark entity pulled Joey off a ladder within ten minutes of his agreeing to help a client dealing with a haunting in his home. After an email consultation where we helped a colleague calm down activity in his house through meditation and warding with salt and iron—activity that included exterior doors mysteriously being opened—we went into our bedroom the next day to find the one window in the room not warded with salt or iron unlocked and open.

Possession

Once a dark entity or entities sufficiently oppress someone, the door is open to *possession*, where the dark entity does not simply work from outside but gets inside the person's body, attaching itself to their energy centers and controlling some or all of the person's personality and actions. Possession is a slippery slope, both because of cultural representations of exorcisms in TV and film and because it shares many symptoms with mental illness. There are those among the clergy and trained by the clergy who can perform exorcisms. In recent years, the Catholic Church alone has trained over 2,000 exorcists to meet the growing demand.

Although we have witnessed both possession and attempted possession in the past few years, we have chosen not to share those cases in this book. The degree of danger and of the need for a specialized team puts possession out of the realm of what we hope to accomplish in this book. For those who are interested, Joey shares these cases in detail in a book he is coauthoring for publication in 2021.

Cynics, Skeptics, and Over-Enthusiasts

Another spectrum of types that we use in our work is also a little different from what everyone else is doing. Joey began considering this trio of personality types while we were running the Webb investigation because—after about a year or so and some seventy or eighty groups of between eight and twenty-five people—we noticed that people's state of mind and relationship to the paranormal, individually and collectively, had a definite effect on the phenomena. We have since been studying the relationship between consciousness and one's experience of the paranormal. It comes into play in many of the cases in this book.

The Cynic

The first type in this triad is the *cynic*. It was always an interesting experience to have a cynic on the Webb investigation. Remember that it was a paid experience and many of our guest investigators were on vacation. A few were there especially to try and debunk the tour and us as investigators—assuming the library was wired up like a funhouse full of special effects, that we were lying, or that we were playing psychological games with them in order to extract information or implant ideas—but thankfully, guests with those intentions were rare. No matter what happened, what the equipment was telling and showing them, and no matter how many people experienced it, the cynics were not going to believe it. We found that ghosts and spirits were less active and communicative when a confirmed cynic was present. This is akin to having the kind of car trouble that only happens when it is not at the mechanic so that it is assumed that somehow you are at fault or mistaken about the condition existing. Cynics call everything into question. Couples, often divided by male and female, sometimes have a cynic and someone who believes. It is a trope in horror films—the tough boyfriend or husband who does not believe his companion until something he cannot explain away finally happens to him. In about one third of our cases, we come across a cynic, usually a member of a family. Although others are experiencing something, they insist they do not. In some instances, they *are* experiencing something, but their fear of it puts their need for logic into overdrive. The "resident cynic" is a trend from the "reality" shows that paranormal investigators and those who request their services should be aware of. They can plant doubt that increases stress and fear, make people feel as though they are becoming unhinged, and create distrust that might prevent people from getting the help they need from credible professionals.

The Over-Enthusiast

On the other end of the triad is the *over-enthusiast*. Again, both at the Webb and during cases, this is rare. Although one might think this is a good thing, it causes as many problems and creates as many obstacles as the cynic. If every creak of the home and every shadow in every picture is a ghost; if every dust speck and lightning bug is an orb; and someone feels like they are constantly being watched, poked, prodded, or followed, then it is hard to take a case history or to separate imagination from true phenomena. Over-enthusiasts also do as much as cynics to affect the experiences of those around them. Nothing creates the conditions for fast-spreading groupthink like the paranormal. The final problem with the over-enthusiast is that they do not respect boundaries. They will go places they are not supposed to, areas where they are not welcome, putting themselves and others at risk, and at times will barrage a spirit or ghost with questions and a lack of respect. Time and again we have experienced ghosts or spirits either stop responding or respond with sarcasm and anger when they have had enough of an over-enthusiast. It is the same as someone shutting their blinds and hiding in their bedroom when a persistent or nosy neighbor is knocking at the door.

The Skeptic

As with the tale of Goldilocks, the middle position is "just right." Joey terms a person with the ability to remain open minded while being rigorous in their testing, research, interpretation, and desire for corroboration a *skeptic*. Skeptic is a word that often gets confused with cynic, which is unfortunate. We welcome skeptics on our investigations and as clients. It makes things easier, safer, and more productive when you know that there is a balance between open-mindedness and looking for alternative explanations. We are still skeptics, even after experiencing all of the things that we report on in our presentations and workshops, on our show and on others, and in our books. Why? Because we have to be realistic—there is still so much we do not know. Just how much of a role does consciousness play? What is really going on with poltergeist activity or with the myriad cryptids and dark entities we encounter? Can these phenomena be accounted for by the existence of parallel dimensions? Skepticism keeps us grounded and showing respect as we continue our exciting but oftentimes frustrating journey of discovery.

Our 10-Point Philosophy (A Paranormal Bill of Rights)

As we were writing this book, we wanted a way to express our philosophy in simple, easily understandable and applicable terms. Over time, we thought about a checklist or set of articles or maxims by which an investigator should abide. Joey thought for sure that, after one hundred and sixty years of paranormal investigation, someone had created one.

When we saw that no one had, we put together the following Paranormal Bill of Rights, with the assistance of some trusted colleagues, who helped us refine the language and ensure that we covered the basics.

This Paranormal Bill of Rights is also at the end of the book. Feel free to remove that page and have it with you when you are doing an investigation or engaging with a haunting in your home or place of business.

Our philosophy is simple:

1. Entities and haunted locations are not specimens or "attractions" to be examined or disturbed at our whim, for our amusement, or to satisfy our curiosity.
2. We ask permission before we enter the space inhabited by an entity or entities.
3. It is not our place to use the tools of our trade to poke, prod, and invade the psychic bodies and minds of entities.

4. We employ the tools of the open-minded skeptic, drawing on past experience and the evidence at hand, while remaining open to new data as it is gathered.

5. At the start of an investigation, we treat entities with respect and we request the same of them.

6. We do not assume that every entity that is unkind, mischievous, or non-communicative is a demon.

7. Under no circumstances do we yell at or threaten entities.

8. In a case where entities are overstepping their bounds, we talk to them—as
you would a partner, neighbor, or coworker—explaining our position and asking them to work with us.

9. We do not believe it is our right to force entities out of a space without first doing a thorough investigation and giving them an opportunity to communicate and be heard.

10. We do not distort this work for attention, financial gain, or to seek power
over any entity. We undertake this work with Humility, Harmony, and Love.

A Few Words Concerning Intention

The human body is a vibrant bioelectric organism pulsating with measurable electrical activity in its cells, neurons, and muscle tissues. For thousands of years, ancient Eastern cultures have recognized this bioelectrical activity as the universal force that animates all living things. In China, it is called *qi* (pronounced chee); in India, it is referred to as *prana*; and in Japan it is called *ki*.

Our universal life force energy is our interface with the unified field and we can direct it with our intention. Because of this, setting a specific intention is extremely important when starting an investigation, or, for that matter, any endeavor. As with any situation, having a clear outcome for your investigation is crucial for results. Our intention when starting an investigation is never to prove anything, but rather, to facilitate help and the highest good for all involved, both living and dead.

In his book, *The Power of Intention,* Dr. Wayne W. Dyer wrote, "Intention is a force in the universe, and everything and everyone is connected to this invisible force."

The unified field of energy connects us all and because of this what we put out through our intention is what we will receive. Holding the intention to learn and assist for every investigation will always yield the best possible outcome for all involved.

We talk about intention again in the final section of this book.

The Tools of Our Trade

In order for us to practice the ten points in the Paranormal Bill of Rights listed above and best live up to our role as responsible skeptics, experiencers, and investigators, we have carefully selected a group of tools for use in our fieldwork.

We revisit some of these tools and introduce you to others in the final section of this book through a slightly different lens—how you can apply them to engaging with or managing a haunting—rather than how we present them here, which focuses on how we developed and have applied them thus far in our practice. We have found this kind of repetition through different lenses to be an invaluable approach to teaching and learning.

Your Body, Senses, and Consciousness are the Best Equipment

This is Tonya's mantra, which she shares with all of our students and at all of our workshops and presentations. The human body is full of biosensors, none of which any of the energy-measuring equipment can match if we understand, develop, and honor them.

During a 1994 United Nations presentation to members of the Society for Enlightenment and Transformation, author, artist, intuitive, and researcher Ingo Swann spoke of these biosensors when he asked, "How many of you here today would like to know you have at least seventeen senses rather than just five of them? How many think that seventeen would be better than just five? How many of you here already know that you have more than five senses?"

Swann followed his question by sharing discoveries made during his years involved in government projects and research, including the discovery of bioelectric sensors not only in the skin, but in the neuropeptide activity that transmits information into the brain and back into the body's extremities, its internal organs, and into its surrounding bioelectromagnetic field. Ingo Swann is known as the father of Remote Viewing, because he, along with physicist Russell Targ, was fundamental in the development of the protocols established by the Stanford Research Institute and the Central Intelligence Agency and delivered to the U.S. military as a training methodology for psychically viewing distant or unseen targets.

Additionally, Swann spoke of what those additional senses are, stating that the soles of our feet and the palms of our hands contain minute magnetic receptors and sensors that "recognize" minute and gross changes in local magnetism.

This means not being so quick to disbelieve as a figment of the imagination what you see and hear. During an investigation or encounter, you want to have those sensors working as openly and clearly as possible. At the same time, you do not want that openness to make you vulnerable to energetic attack. Mastering the balance between an open sensing system and a protected one requires discipline and practice. We are also constantly refining and exploring enhancements to this practice, employing exercises from a broad spectrum of spiritual systems. Tonya's book, *Living the Intuitive Life: Cultivating Extraordinary Awareness*, has exercises that can help.

Other Equipment

One of the areas where investigators differ most widely in philosophy and practice is when it comes to what equipment—and how much of it—to bring on an investigation.

Experience has taught us that less is more. The more equipment, the more expertise and number of team members you require on the technical side of things to manage and make sense of it all. It also means expense and complexity in setting up and analyzing data. You can wind up suffering from *paralysis by analysis*. Plus, the more technology, the greater the possibility of it failing. Spirits, ghosts, and nonhuman entities are energy—we have experienced technology failure on numerous occasions.

With this in mind, and having experimented for a decade in the field, the following pieces of equipment are what we consider to be essential and sufficient:

A digital camera with infrared (to record the investigation and active areas)

A "spirit box" (we prefer the P-SB11)

A digital audio recorder (for EVPs and to have a record of spirit box transmissions) and audio software, such as Audacity

An EMF meter (to detect energy spikes; also can be used for yes/no questions)

A temperature gauge (any drop or rise in temperature more than five degrees without mundane explanation might indicate a presence; we have seen a drop as much as thirteen degrees)

Divining rods and pendulums (great for yes/no questions and if the electronics fail)

It takes hours and abundant patience to go through footage and recordings after an investigation, even with this limited toolkit. Considering that these six pieces of equipment allow us to collect visual and audio recordings, measure temperature and energy levels, and communicate in a number of ways with spirits, ghosts, and other entities, we do not see the need at present to add anything else, although we are always looking at different kinds of technology that are being developed and applied with success.

Cultivate Strong Research Skills

Sherlock Holmes, whose creator, Arthur Conan Doyle, is one of the founders of paranormal research, said: "Data, data, data... I can't make bricks without clay."

In the course of an investigation, we make visits to courthouses, libraries, historical society records rooms and do interviews with locals, librarians, and historians to get context about and insights into the case. We also have an extensive home library of books and multimedia on a wide array of subjects, including firsthand accounts of paranormal phenomena, quantum physics, spiritual systems, and other applicable areas of interest.

We often talk with our older colleagues, whom we respectfully refer to as the Old Guard, about the differences between the early days of UFO investigation in the 1950s and 1960s, when you had to subscribe to newsletters or attend regional and state meetings to get information and today's Technological Age, where abundant information is available on the Internet.

We all agree that, although the Internet is helpful, it still takes corroboration of data from numerous sources to have any confidence in what you are gathering. If you are getting your data solely from electronic sources, you need to do considerable crosschecking. At the end of the day, there is nothing like being on site.

One unquestionable benefit of the Internet is access to UFO reporting sites like the National UFO Reporting Center (NUFORC), founded in 1974 and still maintained by Peter Davenport and the Mutual UFO Network (MUFON). Both are rich sources of data and we have used them extensively when looking at and for patterns and parallels in our investigations.

We have also found a place for social networks in investigating our cases. Like a private investigator or police detective, we are attempting to build a narrative from a set of clues, putting them in context and testing internal coherence of the emerging story as we go. Sites like Facebook can provide information to help solidify the narrative. See the case we call "A Tragic Case of Misidentification in Ohio" later in the book to see how social networking sites aided in our identification and understanding of a tormented ghost.

Knowledge of the geography at or near an investigative site is essential. Landscape, water sources, and geology often come into play. Some areas are considered "hot spots" and may have ley lines, vortexes, portals, or other gateways to parallel dimensions. An understanding of how the energetic grid works is important.

Cultivate the Art and Craft of Interviewing

As paranormal investigators, interviewing is a key and practiced skill. Journalist turned paranormal investigator John Keel said, "Ask the experiencer what they had for breakfast." He was not being literal: he was saying that we need to find out everything we can about the individual's past experiences because he found many were having other experiences that one might not at first connect to an initial UFO encounter or haunting. Some experiencers not only have encounters with ghostly phenomena but also see cryptids, have electronic interference in the home, receive odd phone calls, or report other types of strange visitors.

As you will read in the cases we present in this book, we always start an investigation into a home haunting with at least one interview, where we take a case history and get to know the clients outside of the specific case. This also allows us to identify gaps in the narrative and any internal inconsistencies.

This practice, although it may sound unkind, is essential, because we are mostly dealing with *anecdotal evidence*. In other words, all we have is what people tell us. Individual reports are often difficult to quantify. The credibility of a witness or witnesses may come into question. Some people are lonely and looking for attention. Others watch so many of the paranormal "reality shows" on television that all of their experiences are filtered through that (very distorted) lens. Other experiencers have difficulty describing their experiences because there is nothing with which to compare them. For our part, while interviewing a prospective client, we try to identify certain data bits that we can apply to larger parallels and patterns from reports from different experiencers that do not know each other, or from the literature.

Much of this can only come with practice and the accumulation of experience and the study of the field over time. Having talented mentors is important.

One question that we always ask when assessing anecdotal evidence is: *Why would they lie?*

Given that witnesses to paranormal phenomena have often faced severe ridicule, negativity, and upheaval in their private and professional lives, why do they dare to come forward with their stories? Investigators and researchers are not asking this question enough. Is it for money? Fame? Attention? There is not much evidence for any of these.

For instance, there are the 1966–67 Mothman sightings, which we have been studying for twelve years. Many of the witnesses of the interdimensional being that an enterprising journalist dubbed the "Mothman" left town, underwent divorce, lived in isolation, or otherwise suffered from the weight of negative public opinion from cynics and those who thought they were lying because of paranoia, desire for attention, or mental illness. At an event we attended several years ago, one of the witnesses said that, in the last forty years, he made enough money from his report of a giant bird near to where the Mothman sightings happened to pay his mortgage *for a single month*—hardly sufficient incentive to endure over forty years of scrutiny and ridicule.

We always keep this in mind when interviewing clients. These experiences of the paranormal can be traumatic or life changing or, at the very least, unsettling. We are careful in our questioning not to be perceived as rude or needlessly invasive and we always go in with an open mind.

So, what makes a credible witness? Most people would immediately say pilots, police officers, and those in the military. In many ways, they do have the most to lose and least to gain by coming forward with a report of something paranormal. But, at the same time, we have to ask: What's inherent in those titles that gives them credibility? It could be attention to detail, standing in the community, and the public's respect for a uniform for sure. Also, the high stakes in coming forward, as we said. There are abundant stories of the lives of these respected professionals being ruined. Yet, as responsible investigators, we also know there are plenty of pilots and police officers who are not worthy of our respect and trust and plenty of teenagers and housewives who are.

Of all of the tools in our toolbox, this one is hardest master and also the most important. We are learning all the time.

A Basic Knowledge of Character and Narrative Structure is Essential

Given our life-long experience as writers and actors, it is not surprising that our investigative toolbox includes understanding story. It is helpful when interviewing and assessing anecdotal evidence and in separating Fact from Fiction by looking at context. Anecdotal evidence is like any other data—we need to dissect it so that we can parse out its core elements and structure in order to identify internal inconsistencies. That is what we meant earlier when we talked about "gaps" as well. These are the places where the client may be putting what they experienced through a distorted lens that does not serve the reality of what is happening. This comes into play with several cases in this book.

It is also helpful to understand character-driven traits—what we call motivational and psychological drivers behind a person, spirit, ghost, or entity's Wants and Needs. We cannot do our job well if we do not know what the clients and the entities they are encountering are trying to obtain. This could be, for the client, peace of mind, reclaiming their home, or having someone tell them they are not crazy. For the nonliving, it could be the need to reveal a secret, solve a mystery, or tell their story. Perhaps they need help to process their death and cross over. Or, in the cases of dark entities, what they *need* is to feed on our energy and what they *want* is to provoke fear and despair in order to get it.

Knowing the Value and Limitations of Synchronicity

When seemingly random but unquestionably similar events or experiences occur in close proximity without a discernable, easily identifiable explanation, people often label them *coincidence*, a term that, in our opinion, provides them with a convenient excuse to dismiss without thought things that they do not understand or care to find the deeper meaning of.

Carl Jung believed that coincidences that occur without causality held meaning. He coined the term *synchronicity* to describe these meaningful coincidences. In his book, *Synchronicity: An Acausal Connecting Principle*, Jung wrote:

> [I]t is impossible, with our present resources, to explain ESP, or the fact of meaningful coincidence, as a phenomenon of energy. This makes an end of the causal explanation as well, for 'effect' cannot be understood as anything except a phenomenon of energy. Therefore it cannot be a question of cause and effect, but of a falling together in time, a kind of simultaneity. Because of this quality of simultaneity, I have picked on the term 'synchronicity' to designate a hypothetical factor equal in rank to causality as a principle of explanation.

This "falling together in time" happens frequently during paranormal investigations. Many have direct connection to your investigation, and some do not. Some may be a consequence of having your sensing systems open and your attention sharply focused. Either way, the more they happen, the more you will notice them.

It is those moments, not quite déjà vu, where there is a sense of familiarity or an instance where something you were talking about or working on or thinking about recently appears somewhere else. Joey just experienced one minutes before editing this section. The night before, he started singing like Bing Crosby for no apparent reason. About fifteen hours later, our daughter sent him a few song files he had asked her for and, along with them, she also sent a Bing Crosby song! They had no communication about Bing Crosby prior to the synchronicity occurring.

Sigmund Freud thought this was all simply a matter of something being brought to your attention and then you subsequently seeing or experiencing it for that reason alone. He was partially right. That does of course happen. But many spiritual and psychological practitioners believe that synchronicity is an essential part of being in tune with your surroundings, materially and energetically.

Joey catalogs his synchronicities and we find that they can sometimes be helpful while on an investigation. For *Watch Out for the Hallway*, we determined that only a dozen synchronicities experienced over the course of two years/150 hours were important enough to understanding what is happening at the Webb and how the paranormal affects our consciousness to warrant mention. By applying rigorous examination to synchronicities as you do to other data, you can tease out "mere coincidence" from data indicating design and patterns—things to which you should be paying attention.

Like anything else, synchronicity can be overused and wrongly interpreted as significant, but used correctly it a legitimate addition the toolbox.

Over the course of the book, we call your attention to important synchronicities we experienced in some of our homes and while investigating the reported cases.

Transdisciplinarity and the Quest for Parallels and Patterns

Transdisciplinarity, or the breaking down of the walls that compartmentalize PhD/specialist thinking in academia and scientific investigation, was first popularized by quantum physicist Basarab

Nicolescu in the 1980s, although a decade earlier Swiss psychologist Jean Paget was the one who coined the term.

Transdisciplinarity is a central feature of our investigative philosophy. We have studied for two decades to have a functional understanding of the basics of quantum physics; neuroscience; consciousness studies; dream interpretation, symbolism, and mythology/folklore; energy healing; anthropology; shamanism; and human psychology.

Transdisciplinarity is how we came to define the part of our approach to paranormal investigation that we call *Conditional Anomalous Phenomena* (CAP). We work hard to find mundane, traditionally scientific explanations for what is experienced rather than assume at the outset that what we are investigating is paranormal in origin. Applying the array of tools we use to identify CAP, we can serve as our own debunkers. This is always preferable to doing sloppy, incomplete work and having someone else point it out.

Because the origin and "truth" of the paranormal and supernatural are not currently knowable, a large percentage of the data that we collect resides under the umbrella of CAP. Most responsible investigators and researchers would say the same.

We always keep in mind that Correlation is not always Causation and having a working knowledge of the fields listed above strengthens our ability to apply this principle to our investigations. Nontraditional science is beginning to formulate alternative explanations for the linear and three-dimensional models of Time and Space that traditional science has long put forth. The more current our knowledge of these fast-changing fields, the better able we are to separate CAP from actual phenomena and to successfully understand a haunting.

The following paragraphs talk a little more about some of these fields and the role they play in our work.

Role of the observer. During investigations, the background/psychology of the observer informs the case. We rise to our labels. The same goes for clients. You will see many instances in this book of people who made a bad situation worse (or a good situation bad) by not understanding how they were affecting the phenomena because of their worldview and presuppositions.

Consciousness studies. Recent mainstream research says human consciousness survives after death. When you compare ancient texts like the Upanishads, the work of Emmanuel Swedenborg and John Dee, and other mystical, esoteric, and spiritual texts, it is clear that mystics, intuitives, and nontraditional thinkers have understood this from the onset. Traditional science is finally catching up.

In addition, research in the field of neuroscience has revealed the existence of a "unified field of consciousness" that is distinct, meaning that the observer, the observed, and the process of observation are one.

Perhaps this new understanding about the nature of consciousness indicates that quantum mechanics, the rules governing the physical world at the subatomic level, play an important role in consciousness. Physicist and author John Hagelin has claimed that consciousness comes from the higher dimensions, and, in fact, is the "ground of all being."

Exciting research by some well-respected scientists shows that consciousness does not depend on the brain and may, in fact, survive the death of our bodies. The possibility of life after death is a long-debated topic; however, British physicist Sir Roger Penrose believes that he and his research team have found evidence that protein-based microtubules carry quantum information that is stored at a subatomic level.

Penrose has stated, "If they're not revived, and the patient dies, it's possible that this quantum information can exist outside the body, perhaps indefinitely, as a soul."

Continuing research in the fields of quantum mechanics and consciousness research may soon provide compelling explanations for such phenomena as ghosts and hauntings.

The ancient spiritual texts we referred to earlier also overlap with the fundamental tenets of quantum physics, as explained in Fritof Capra's *The Tao of Physics*, Michael Talbot's *Mysticism and the New Physics*, and other seminal books on the nexus of these once-disparate fields. Given that spirits, ghosts, and nonhuman entities are made of energy, this area of study is essential for us to understand.

Given the mounting evidence, both anecdotal and scientific, that astral travel, time slips, phasing in and out of our "reality," channeling, psychic questing, psychic attacks, and possession are real, *transdisciplinarity* assesses how they fit into the larger parallels and patterns.

We believe it is our best hope for understanding them.

It's now time to take all we have talked about in these introductory sections and apply them to homes in which we have lived over the past two decades and cases on which we have worked.

Part I: Our Haunted Homes

Mesa, Arizona (Tonya's story)

In 1996, I moved with my two young sons to a split-level house in Mesa, Arizona. Daniel was eleven and Jeremy had just turned two. On our first night in the house, I began having bizarre nightmares about demonic-type creatures entering through my bedroom window and roaming through the house. I would wake up drenched in sweat and terrified.

The house had a sublevel family room, which the boys loved because it was spacious and made a terrific playroom. From the start, Daniel complained of an uneasy feeling and the sense that he was being watched, especially when he was in the family room. One night not long after we moved in, Daniel was downstairs in the family room playing a game on his computer when out of the corner of his eye he saw the apparition of an old woman cross the room to the left of him. She faded away as he turned to look at her full on. He described her to me as "hag-like" and "menacing."

On several occasions I found Jeremy standing at the foot of the staircase, pointing upstairs and repeating the word "scary." One night I was watching television in the living room, which was on the ground floor. The stairs leading down to the family room were just to the left of the sofa and I could hear Jeremy playing and murmuring to someone (whom I assumed was Daniel) at the bottom of the stairs. I didn't think much of it—I thought it was just part of whatever he and Daniel were playing. As I continued to listen, however, something about Jeremy's voice sounded odd, so I strained to hear better what he was saying. I suddenly realized that it was, "Help me, help me!" I ran downstairs and found him in a facedown position at the bottom of the staircase, unable to move and barely able any longer to make his plea for help. Daniel had been around the corner playing on his computer with his headphones on and hadn't heard Jeremy, nor had he been the one talking to Jeremy a few minutes before. I scooped Jeremy up and carried him up the stairs, and as I did, he pointed to the top of the stairs and said again, "Scary."

The nightmares and the strange sensation of someone watching us continued and grew more vivid, and a strange reddish substance began to appear on the walls and near the ceiling in the bedrooms, for which I could find no explanation.

The final straw came one afternoon when Daniel was at school. Jeremy was taking a nap and I was in the bathroom getting ready for work. As I leaned toward the mirror to apply my mascara, I heard a sinister witch-like cackle so close to me that I felt a cold breath in my ear. This unsettled me so much that I ran into Jeremy's bedroom, picked him up, and headed quickly down the stairs. I could feel us *move through something I could not see*. It was a sensation I had never experienced before, nor have I since, despite a decade of investigating and communicating with nonliving beings. It is hard to describe—it was as if the air was thicker, colder, and had actual substance in that particular spot. I took Jeremy to my parents and began making plans to move out of the house. I remember thinking that I wished there was a way to locate someone who might know how to investigate what was going on and provide some assistance. Keep in mind—this was in the days before the Internet connected us more easily to nontraditional people and organizations and before paranormal shows and groups were really a "thing." Little did I know that I would be cowriting a book to offer the type of assistance I was unable to find then over twenty years later!

Brick Township, New Jersey

In the summer of 2000, we moved our family of five into a spacious two-bedroom apartment in Brick Township, New Jersey. This was the beginning of our shared experiences with the paranormal—experiences that have now continued for nearly twenty years. Looking back, we can say that the apartment in Brick was a sort of "paranormal starter kit" for us as a family. Nothing was dangerous or even persistent, except for instances of sleep paralysis that we detail at the end of this section. Overall, our experiences there helped to make us aware that there is more to the world than what scientists allow.

During our nearly five years in this apartment, we experienced strange, and sometimes humorous, occurrences. We discovered early on that finding humor in the Unknown whenever you can is a valuable and important tool because it helps diminish the fear that comes with facing things we don't completely understand.

It all started with a smell. Like most families, we would all gather in the living room after dinner to watch television, play video games, read, or converse. At least a few times a week, a strange odor would manifest right next to us, seemingly out of nowhere. The odor was distinctly that of a person who was in desperate need of a shower. Because our two sons, like many pre-teen boys, weren't always great about hygiene, we at first thought it was one of them, but it quickly became clear that it wasn't.

Whenever the odor started, it would linger anywhere from a few minutes to a few hours and then vanish as quickly as it manifested. It would also move around the room, as if whoever—or whatever—it was attached to was changing position in the room. Try as we might, we were never able to identify its source. Because it was more of an annoyance than a frightful experience, we would usually just matter-of-factly comment that the "stinky man" was back whenever this phenomenon occurred and laugh it off as weird.

Our daughter Jolie, who was an active, precocious two-year-old, seemed to be tuned into and able to see other activity that was occurring in the apartment. She would often point and ask who was walking down the hallway when she and Tonya were the only ones at home. On one such occasion she insisted that she had just seen her brother Jeremy walk down the hallway toward their bedroom although Jeremy was at school.

One afternoon, Tonya was alone in the apartment washing dishes when she felt something lightly tap her heels. She looked down to see Jolie's bouncy ball, which had been sitting quite still in front of the sofa the last she had seen it. For the ball to reach her feet, it would have had to roll at least eight feet and make turns around two sharp corners.

Once, while she was (again) doing the dishes, Jolie came in from the living room and insisted that there was an old man on the couch. Tonya ran into the living room and found the couch—and the room—empty. We were so new at experiencing the paranormal we never thought to correlate the "stinky old man" smell with the ghost of the old man Jolie saw. It would have been an easy enough thing to contact our landlord, with whom we were on excellent terms, and ask if an older man had lived in the apartment before we did.

One afternoon, as Tonya was taking a nap on the couch where Jolie saw the old man, she found herself floating in a liminal space. She was not awake or asleep but fully aware of the room around her. It was as if she could see the living room although her eyes were closed. As she was noticing this, she began to see and hear a number of people walking through the living room and walking past the sofa. It was as if a location with a high volume of foot traffic from another dimension had been overlaid onto the space of our living room. This lasted for several minutes before she returned to consciousness.

Sleep paralysis was a common occurrence for Tonya during our years in that apartment. Each experience of sleep paralysis was preceded by a lucid dream in which she was lying in our bed and looking around the room. Just as in the classic reports of sleep paralysis, she would then experience the sensation of a sinister presence in the room, usually hovering right over her. In a state of terror, and unable to move, she would struggle to open her eyes and wake up, but it was not to be. These episodes would last several minutes before she would finally find a way to force herself awake.

In addition to sleep paralysis, having particularly vivid dreams was another common occurrence for us both at this time, which coincided with the start of our intensive study of spirituality, different healing modalities, and conscious dreaming and astral travel. During the four years that we lived in that apartment we both kept extensive dream journals. Years later, we began to realize that many of the dreams we had during that time were prophetic. In fact, as we were working on the first draft of this book in early spring 2020, during the Coronavirus lockdown, we were revisiting those journals and discovered uncanny similarities between some of those dreams and the events that were unfolding around us during the early months of the pandemic.

Because we are committed to reminding people as often as we can that not all paranormal experiences are evil, dark, or dangerous, we have to say again that, with the exception of the sleep paralysis episodes, we were fortunate that nothing that we experienced while living in that apartment was particularly unsettling or terrifying. Unfortunately, what we were about to experience in our next home would take our paranormal experiences to a completely new and at times frightening level.

Tinton Falls, New Jersey

As strange as the phenomena in the Brick apartment were, they did little to prepare us for what we were about to experience as we were attempting to settle into and make for ourselves a home in Tinton Falls. We choose these words carefully because, although it was our place of residence for nearly a year, it never did feel like home. There were active forces there that made sure it never would. It was a place where we, our children, and our adult housemate and business partner experienced persistent manifestation, infestation, and oppression.

It was, at the time, the closest we had ever come to living in a classic haunted house.

In December 2004, we moved into a cozy two-bedroom Cape Cod on a quiet street in Tinton Falls, New Jersey. We had to convert an additional two rooms into bedrooms to accommodate the five of us who were going to inhabit the space. Not only would two of our children be living there with us, we had decided to share space with Joey's friend since high school, whom we had just opened an acting school and rehearsal space for our theatre company with. With so much to do, we knew we would be spending an immense amount of time together and sharing a house was a way to control costs while freeing up capital to invest in the business.

Our two children were more than happy with the arrangement. In the Italian tradition, they called some of our closest male friends "uncle" out of respect, and this one in particular was like a godfather to them.

The search for the perfect house for five people was time-consuming, so we were all relieved and excited when we found this beautiful home with a newly remodeled kitchen and a layout that allowed for both privacy as well as inviting and functional common areas. There was also a big backyard where we had several parties and barbeques. We also had a garden and a row of eight-foot-tall sunflowers. Sound idyllic? Because in many ways, especially at the start, it was.

However, just like with the trope of the couple or family who move into a new house in order to make a clean start after a period of turmoil or to live out their dreams, the idyllic home we tried to make soon became a place of fear. In fact, from the very first day it seemed as if bad experiences would overshadow our time in that house. They started as minor *manifestations*—inconveniences really, mostly mundane—but it did not take long for the phenomena to ramp up to *infestation*.

The first day, looking back, really was a foreshadowing of things to come. Of course, at the time, we had barely begun our spiritual training and were in no way adept at interpreting the now obvious warning signs we were getting right from the start. We moved in on a cold, rainy December day and when we arrived with the moving truck, we discovered that the master bedroom, located in the finished basement, had badly flooded due to a failed water heater. The damage was so bad that we and our two children had to stay with Joey's family for several weeks so the water could be extracted, any signs of mold mitigated, and the carpet replaced. Our business partner, who was originally supposed to have his bedroom in the basement, moved into the converted attic space that was going to be our bedroom.

Once the work in the basement was finally complete, we began unpacking and settling in. A few days later, we noticed a thin black film covering everything in the basement. We had no idea what it was. We would wipe it off, only to find it would return in a day or so, just as pervasive as before. After several days of having to clean it up, the oil furnace suddenly stopped working, so we called an HVAC repairman to come and take a look.

Tonya will never forget the look on the repairman's face when she opened the door upon his arrival. The kids were at school and

Joey and our business partner were off on separate appointments. She thought it was odd and more than a bit unsettling the way the repairman seemed to glare at her as she said hello and thanked him for coming. His expression was so penetrating, in fact, that as she led him downstairs to the furnace she wondered if he was going to be ill mannered and difficult to deal with.

As Tonya showed him the furnace in the back room of the basement, he startled her with his questions, which had nothing to do with the heating system. First, he asked about her grandmother Clara (by name!) while assuring Tonya she was with her almost all the time. He asked who in the house was writing about knights and dragons, a reference to Joey's first novel (which he was revising at the time), and he went on to describe Joey in detail, whom he had obviously never met. The repairman (whom we refer to here as Jack in homage to the F. Paul Wilson novels) went on to explain that he was a psychic medium and that he could see that, like Clara, Tonya also had the "gift." Jack then offered to come by the house on evenings and weekends to help her develop her natural abilities.

After inspecting the heating system, Jack found that there was nothing wrong with it except a missing filter, which was the reason for the black soot we were finding. Jack's discovery may have saved us from carbon monoxide poisoning. The heater malfunction was so curious that we were confident that someone, perhaps Tonya's grandmother, had been looking out for us, causing the furnace to stop functioning although, mechanically, it was fine.

As Jack was leaving, our business partner pulled into the driveway. Jack approached him and told him not to feel bad about something that he had witnessed when he was just a boy. His guilt was unnecessary. There was nothing he could have done. Our business partner was unsettled, understandably, by the exchange. Jack had gotten all of the details correct—and it was something our business partner never spoke about to us. Jack also cautioned him to watch his speed—he had a habit of driving too fast and it was going to get him into trouble.

Jack returned a few weeks later to begin working with Tonya, but by then there was so much persistent activity in the house (*infestation*) that she was more interested in having him do a reading to identify what was going on than starting lessons in mediumship.

Tonya led him through the house and shared what we had been experiencing room by room.

They began in Jeremy's bedroom. Tonya explained that Jeremy had been complaining that every morning around 3 am he would wake up to his stereo or ceiling fan turning on by itself. One morning Jeremy awoke to find that, not only was his ceiling fan on, there were two people on his television— *which was turned off*. The scene he saw was something out of a horror film and nothing a 10-year-old should ever be subjected to—a man choking a young woman. It frightened him so badly he spent the night on the living room couch.

After spending several minutes in Jeremy's bedroom but not doing anything but listening, Jack asked Tonya to take him into our daughter Jolie's room. Jolie was four at the time and had begun to experience terrible nightmares on a nightly basis, something she had never experienced previously, but something that then continued well into her teens. Jolie had reported to us that she had seen a black mass floating toward the living room one night, and Tonya shared with Jack how we often experienced a sense of uneasiness accompanied by the feeling of someone watching us while in the living room. Jolie had also started experiencing headaches almost daily. She had never complained of headaches before moving into the house and they started almost immediately after moving in. Since she was only four at the time, and otherwise healthy, the sudden onset of headaches was *idiopathic*, meaning the cause was unknown.

In line with many reports of paranormal phenomena, 3 am was not just a strange time for Jeremy. We were also experiencing strange phenomena at what many call the "witching hour" or the "hour of the wolf." Almost every morning at that time, the telephone would ring, yet there was never anybody on the line. When we answered, we would often hear a series of clicks, beeps, or static; sometimes there would be nothing except silence. This is another trope of hauntings and reports of paranormal phenomena. Going all the way back to the invention of the telephone in 1876, people have been reporting these kinds of calls. A Newark, New Jersey funeral parlor owner's life began to fall apart in 1878 when he had a phone installed in his home so he could call into his business rather than go back and forth. Every night at 4 am he and his wife would be awakened by the phone ringing, without anyone being there.

As a means of privacy, we had hung a beaded curtain at the foot of the stairs leading to our basement bedroom. We often heard the curtain swinging as though someone had walked through it, in conjunction with the phantom phone calls.

As Tonya and Jack exited Jolie's room, she shared how we would often hear footsteps in conjunction with what sounded like a heavy ball bouncing across the floor in the third-floor bedroom (where our business partner slept) when nobody was up there. She explained that on several occasions she had heard the voices of children coming from the basement when she was home alone.

Finally, Tonya shared with Jack the encounters that, more than any of the other experiences, had left us with the desire to move our family to a safer, more peaceful house. The first occurred one afternoon as Tonya was standing in front of the bedroom mirror applying makeup. Suddenly she noticed in the reflection a being with a hog's face and tusks standing behind her and just over her right shoulder. It was a humanoid figure dressed in a blue military jacket with yellow, fringed epaulettes. Tonya turned around and found no one there. The encounter was so odd and happened so quickly she dismissed it, deciding to keep it to herself.

Two days later, the second encounter occurred. Joey had arrived home just before dinner and went down to our bedroom to change and check email before joining the family in the kitchen. Before he reached the bottom of the stairs, Tonya, who was by the stove, heard him let out a terrified scream before scrambling back up the stairs and into the kitchen. What he described reminded Tonya of the importance of trusting her experiences. Joey explained that, as he neared the bottom of the staircase and parted the beaded curtain, he saw a greenish-blue, glowing hog's head staring up at him from where it hovered a foot off the ground.

After Tonya related these experiences to Jack, he explained that he felt that what we were experiencing was poltergeist activity, perhaps brought on by Jeremy approaching puberty and the stress of the move and new business, and that it soon would pass. After assuring Tonya that we had nothing to worry about, he left and we never heard from him again. Tonya called him a few times to see if he was still interested in coming to help her develop her skills as a medium, but her calls were never returned.

Tonya's grandma Clara had taught her enough about poltergeists to know that our experiences in that house did not fit the criteria for such activity. We felt confident that Jack was not comfortable sharing with us what he had actually sensed in the house, and had made the choice to downplay the activity in an attempt to ease our concerns. That we never heard from him again convinced us that whatever it was that he sensed in the house had instilled in him the desire not to return, nor did he want to be around it or enlighten us to the truth.

As you will read later, he was not the only one to keep the secrets of what might really being going on in that house—and neighborhood—from us.

Poltergeist is a German word that means "noisy ghost" and is a phenomenon that usually involves loud noises such as banging or knocking, frequently accompanied by objects such as chairs moving around, or even through the air as if being thrown. There has been a lot of research done over the centuries with regard to this phenomenon, which became a household word due to the popularity of the 1982 film that bears its name. Many researchers believe it to be the result of human psychokinesis (the ability to affect matter with the mind, often times subconsciously) rather than the actions of malevolent spirits. Jack was right in one respect—poltergeist activity tends to center on teenagers, particularly females, and psychical researchers theorize that emotional and hormonal changes produce a type of uncontrolled psychokinesis. Some characteristic traits of poltergeist activity are that it often only occurs when the angsty teen is present, and the activity tends to stop as abruptly as it begins.

Because all five of us were being woken up almost nightly as a result of the phenomena we have reported so far, five months or so into the experience we were all suffering in our own ways from irritability, lack of focus, and even depression.

The activity had progressed from *infestation* to *oppression*.

Before we continue with more of the phenomena generated by the house in Tinton Falls, we want to mention that, although it is an inescapable fact that starting a new business, especially in the arts, comes with abundant stressors, including a tight budget, and that we were all learning to live together, these factors do not account for the severity of the mood changes we were all undergoing.

Here is an example. One afternoon, something occurred between Joey and our business partner that led to the realization that the house was having a negative impact on our moods and our behavior to a dangerous degree. What started as a difference of opinion—about something minor—quickly escalated into a prolonged screaming match. As they argued, the two men stood well apart in the kitchen, with the dining table serving as a barrier between them, because the vibe was one of impending physical violence. At the apex of the argument, Joey's friend stormed upstairs to his room. From the kitchen Joey could hear the unmistakable sound of several glass items breaking in the bedroom above.

Although they were at the time a couple of hotheaded Italian Americans who were as close as brothers and sometimes fought like them, this was not the kind of intense behavior either of them had ever displayed with each other. Fifteen years later, they are still close.

As to our marriage, it was not faring any better. The problems with the house, the difficulties the kids were having, and the 3 am calls were making a good night's sleep increasingly rare and we began getting on each other's nerves. One day, while Tonya was out, Joey found her engagement, wedding, and five-year anniversary bands on her nightstand. The oppression the activity in the house was causing, which manifested as fatigue and agitation, led him to believe that it was a not-so-subtle message about her changing feelings for him. Therefore, he took the trio of rings and hid them in a porcelain theatre mask hung on a three-inch nail on the 4 inch × 4 inch oak beam that ran the length of their bedroom ceiling.

Arriving home a few hours later, Tonya went downstairs to retrieve her rings, which she had innocently forgotten. While she was out, she had been worried that she may have lost them. Joey was on the far side of the room, working on his computer when Tonya asked him if he had seen her rings. He played dumb, but quickly began to press her for why she had gone out without wearing them. They started to argue. As they did, the theatre mask *lifted off* the nail and, as it fell to the floor, the three rings came flying out of the mask and landed on the bed, which was *behind* where the mask had been hanging. As the mask fell, it appeared to be happening in slow motion, the porcelain mask slowly projecting *forward* as the rings projected *backward*.

One is hard pressed to explain that happening using any traditional principles of physics. At best, the mask would have fallen straight down to the floor and the rings might have remained inside—the bottom of the mask was at least three inches deep.

After this incident our housemate had an unsettling incident where, returning home from a wedding one weekend while we were away, he found himself locked in the bathroom as his cat became increasingly agitated outside the door. Twenty minutes later, the cat settled down and the door opened without trouble.

By that point, we had certainly had enough. The oppression was worsening.

Something had to be done.

Not knowing where else to turn (Jack had long since disappeared), we contacted Joey's aunt and uncle, who were extensively trained spiritual healers and counselors. They quickly agreed to come to the house and arrived within a few days.

After spending several hours with us, but not saying much, they got in their car and returned home. The next day, Joey's aunt, a to-the-point Italian-American Roman Catholic with an unwavering devotion to family, called him and said, "Here's what I think. It is not just your house that's haunted—it's the entire block. Buy out your lease, take a financial loss, do whatever you have to—but get your family out of there."

It was roughly a week later, with our still being uncertain about what we should do, that a decision was forced on us—a not uncommon occurrence in these types of cases. At 3 am (note the time) a valve on the hot water heater burst, flooding the basement for a second time. Although there was nothing paranormal about an old hot water heater failing, this was the final straw. We could not ignore the time of night—3 am. It was at this point that we arranged for Tonya and the kids to stay with Joey's parents until we could secure new living arrangements. The landlord, embarrassed by the endless troubles with the house and confident that she had a buyer for the property, let us out of our lease a month early without penalty and our housemate moved out soon after.

After staying with Joey's parents for a short while, we rented a small, overpriced townhouse that strained our bottom line, a situation we knew would be only a temporary fix. Although we did not have any paranormal experiences there, the exhaustion and oppression we had suffered had taken their toll. Worn out by the financial and logistical challenges of living in New Jersey in the aftermath of 9/11, we decided it was time to offer the kids a more relaxed pace of life. After we had considered several potential states, a close friend offered us an opportunity to purchase three acres in the quiet West Virginia countryside.

At the end of the one-year lease of the townhouse we sold our business partner our share of the theatre school and prepared for our new adventure.

Fairmont, West Virginia (aka "The Holler")

Merriam-Webster's online dictionary defines a hollow as "a depressed or low part of a surface, especially a small valley or basin." In the American South, particularly in the Southern Appalachians and Ozarks, native inhabitants pronounce hollow as "holler," and we happily began following suit even before we moved.

Tucked into the hillside of a West Virginia holler, our newly built home was a vision of serenity and promised to provide us with the lifestyle we had envisioned for our family of five (our oldest son had decided to move back home) after many years of searching for the perfect fit. In fact, the picturesque country setting was so promising that Joey gave our new home the nickname "New Walton's Mountain" as an homage to the popular TV series about a tight-knit, well-grounded family.

Our move, however, was not without its challenges. While we coordinated from eight hours away all of the testing that needed to be done on the land for things like the septic system (the first test failed so our 1.5 acre plan doubled to 3 acres when all was said and done), our builder went out of business with virtually no warning. We then had to scramble to work with our mortgage company to find a new builder that could come close to our original floorplan while meeting budget and schedule restraints. Although we had to compromise in several areas, we were overall thrilled with how the house turned out.

The debacle that was our actual move, from the moving company arriving eight hours late, to their leaving Joey and our son in the middle of nowhere near midnight with no idea of how to get to the house where we were temporarily staying when we finally arrived in West Virginia, to the truck breaking down as they tried to drive it up our steep, three hundred and fifty foot gravel driveway the next day, is a 48-hour horror story we told in detail for many years.

Some houses resist you moving in, and others won't let you go.

The Holler house did both.

When we arrived in West Virginia, the challenges continued. Due to a dispute between the person who sold us the land and two brothers that owned dozens of acres on either side of us, the electric company had not received the permissions needed to run service to our house. After unloading the moving truck into the unfinished basement, we stayed with friends whose house was just across the holler from us as we waited for the situation to be resolved. Delay after delay extended our stay with our neighbors for nearly a month while our belongings got wet because of an incomplete window installation in the basement. The water damage was so bad that we lost thousands of dollars of property to mold.

To ease our mounting frustration, one afternoon we decided to take a walk and explore the holler. We descended the hill behind our neighbor's house and stopped to explore an area near a mound in the holler basin. As we did, we came across a stand of trees, in the center of which was an old, gnarled tree trunk. We were delighted to observe, tucked into the moss-covered wood, what could only be described as a miniature faerie village.

Although no faeries were present, we could see the dwellings and features of the village and Joey was convinced that they would emerge within moments. The scene was so pristine and perfectly interwoven into the indigenous plant life that Joey suggested Tonya take a picture of it. As Tonya raised her camera, however, the idyllic vision instantly vanished and left us staring at a dead tree wrapped in rusted barbed wire, surrounded by old cinder blocks and a variety of trash. We believe that we witnessed, for just a few moments, something out of time and space. It would not be the last time a portal or other interdimensional doorway opened in that area.

When the problem with the electric was finally resolved, Joey suggested that Tonya and the kids start staying in the house while final touches were completed. Because the Internet was yet to be connected, Joey needed to stay behind so he could continue to work. Although tensions from an unexpected, prolonged stay with friends were rising, Tonya was reluctant. She found herself feeling uneasy in the house from the start. Throughout the house, there was an overwhelming sense of someone watching her, particularly in the master bedroom.

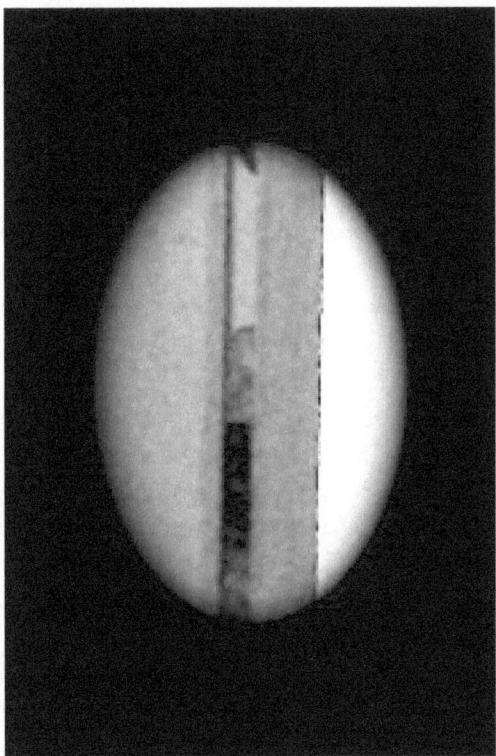

As Tonya and the kids settled in, odd things began to happen (*manifestation*). Strange noises were a regular occurrence, particularly in Jolie's bedroom. Doors would often close by themselves. "Faerie lights" would appear in the house and later on the property, starting small and growing in size, sometimes as big as a beach ball, before fading away. Tonya would frequently wake in the middle of the night to the sound of banging, often in a series of three knocks, against the back of the house.

One afternoon, during a nap, she woke to see the figure of a little girl standing beside the bed. Not long after, she decided to take photos in the master bedroom when she felt the spirit was present. In one of the photos, what appears to be the face of a young girl is seen peeking through the closet door, which had been slightly ajar. [see photo] Tonya was alone in the bedroom at the time she took the photo.

The little girl told her story to Tonya through a dream one afternoon during another nap.

In the dream, a blonde pioneer girl of about ten was hopelessly trying to find her way back to her homestead. After wandering for hours through the woods, she gave into exhaustion, and lay down next to a tree, located next to a large boulder, where she died. Tonya instantly recognized the tree and boulder as the same tree and boulder at the top of our driveway.

Several months later, Tonya was receiving a reading from a psychic who, without Tonya mentioning her, brought up the little girl, whom he said had attached herself to Tonya, having become quite fond of her. He also pointed out that the girl thought Joey was much too serious (which was true) and she loved to play practical jokes on him by hiding items like his keys, to get him to lighten up a little.

This was also true—small objects belonging to Joey would frequently disappear, particularly his keys, and usually when he was getting ready to leave to go to a meeting in town.

During our years in the holler house, Tonya experienced many psychic and paranormal visitations through dreams. The dreams frequently focused on the area between two walnut trees, located directly in front of the house. Our good friend and mentor, Rosemary Ellen Guiley, later confirmed during an investigation of our property what we had surmised all along—that the area, especially the space between the walnut trees, was a portal.

Each of Tonya's dreams connected to the portal area began the same way. Tonya would be staring out the window into the portal location. In one such dream, Tonya noticed a Cro-Magnon humanoid was picking plants in that area. Moments later, Jolie was in the yard with him and Tonya screamed for Jolie to come inside, away from the man. Unrattled, Jolie took the Cro-Magnon's hand and led him to the front porch, where the man shapeshifted into a modern-looking senior with grey hair and glasses. The man introduced himself as George Washington, raising Tonya's suspicions, although, as a young man, Washington had been a surveyor in what was then western Virginia, especially near to Point Pleasant, which would soon begin to call to us to come for a visit and an experience that would change our lives forever.

Back to the dream. Tonya, fearing for Jolie's safety, pulled her inside and closed the door. The dream then ended.

Dreams within dreams were another common occurrence. A month after the Cro-Magnon dream, Tonya dreamed that she woke from a dream and sat up in her bed. She glanced toward the bedroom window and spotted an American Indian boy peering into the bedroom. Tonya ran to the window and the boy ran to the portal area. Tonya opened the front door and called out to the boy who made his way to the porch, at which point his head transformed into that of a giant mole. Tonya grabbed his snout and then she woke up.

Another dream within a dream occurred during another afternoon nap. In the dream, Tonya had just awoken from a bout of sleep paralysis and lay in bed, relieved that she was able to move. She looked out the window, where she observed three American Indians performing a ceremony in a circle. Curious, she rose to go investigate. On her way to the front door, she encountered a small, blue man, approximately three feet tall, with pointy ears. The man was grinning and Tonya asked him his name. "Philolexi!" he responded. Tonya invited him to sit and tell her about himself and his people and he made his way to the armchair and climbed up. Just as he started to talk, Tonya awakened. Rosemary was staying with us this particular afternoon, and had just gifted Tonya with a copy of her latest book titled, *Fairies: Mysteries, Folklore, and Fact* (now out of print). Tonya and Rosemary had been discussing the book prior to taking an afternoon nap, and Tonya is sure that Rosemary's presence and the conversation about faeries served to create the perfect opportunity for a visit from their realm.

Her dream encounter with Philolexi also led Tonya to wonder if it had been his voice she had heard months earlier while doing dishes. She was alone in the house that day and, as she stood at the sink, her hands submerged in dishwater, Tonya heard a tiny, high-pitched voice exclaim, "Not *meeee!*" Baffled as to where the voice had come from, Tonya searched the house and found nothing.

It is possible that Philolexi was a kobold, which is a species of supposedly mythological house spirits that folklorists say are ambivalent. Considering Tonya was doing the dishes and he did not cause her any harm—nor did he offer to help (was that the meaning of "Not *meeee!*"?)—it's a pretty good guess.

Speaking of small, supernatural beings, encounters with faeries became a regular part of our life in the holler. As we mentioned, others (including several paranormal investigators) also frequently observed faerie lights moving around the property—at times, as we mentioned, as large as a beach ball—and often right through the middle of our living room. One morning near the large tree that the pioneer girl had revealed in her dream, Tonya noticed a perfect circle of flowers. In the center, the grass was short and sparse, a stark contrast to the long weeds growing outside the ring. In Celtic lore, such an anomaly is known as a faerie ring and is believed to be a favored location for faeries to gather and dance.

Next to that tree sat the large flat-topped boulder beside which the little girl had died. The boulder became a favorite place for us and the kids to sit when we sought to meditate in solitude and commune with nature. Joey would read books and journal on that rock for hours. The energy of the area under that tree and near the boulder was apparent not just to our family, but also to the family who had just built a house on the hill behind our property. One afternoon, while their house was under construction, Joey observed several women in burkas descend from the hilltop and stop at the boulder, where they appeared to be praying and offering a blessing.

Tonya would often leave offerings near the faerie ring and on the boulder for the faeries. One spring after the snow had melted, Joey was outside when he noticed twelve white stones arranged in a

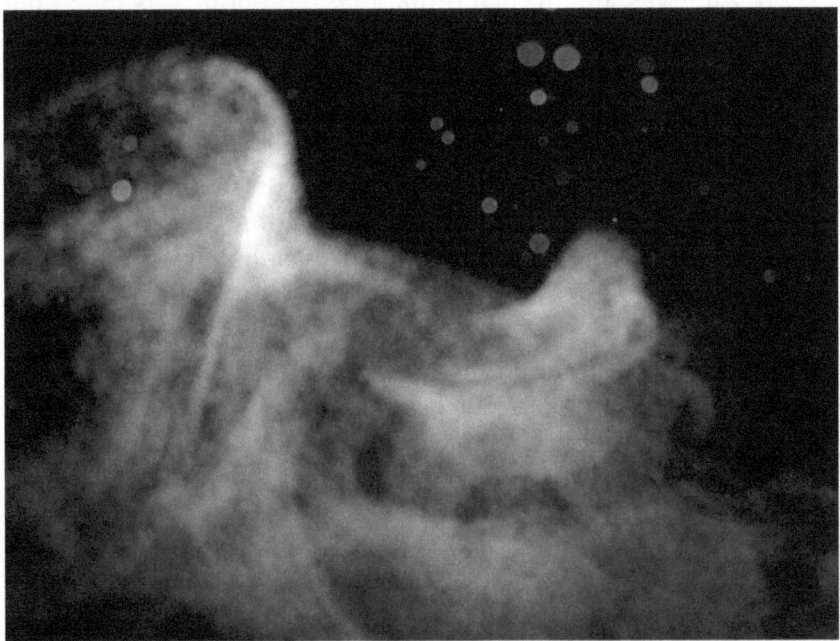

pattern along the boulder [see photo]. Each oval stone was pristine and white and measured about an inch. The boulder was buried under layers of snow all winter and the snow had just melted away. No one in the house had placed them there. This led Joey to believe that the faeries had left the stones as a gift several weeks earlier. He has kept them either on an altar in his writing room or in a velvet bag ever since.

In addition to dreams, waking manifestations became a common occurrence. In October 2010, Tonya had been taking photos of the fall decorations adorning the front deck and hung around the house. One afternoon while examining the photos on her digital camera, Tonya's attention was drawn to a photo that made no sense. Although she had not taken any photos for several days, there was a photo dated the previous day that appeared to be of a misty apparition floating in darkness. A plethora of orbs surrounded the apparition and she could clearly make out a face. The misty form reminded Tonya and others of a nun in a habit [see photo].

Finding no explanation as to how the photo had appeared on the camera, she emailed it to paranormal researcher and author Brad Steiger for his opinion. Steiger sent the photo to his photographic expert who was able to determine that the photo was taken outside. He said that it appeared to be ectoplasm. The specialist went on to say that if Tonya had not taken the photo it had been placed there by a spirit to show proof of its existence.

The photo would not be Tonya's only experience with strange mists there. One afternoon, as she drove down the winding, gravel road that descended into the holler, Tonya noticed a black mist in the sky hovering just above our house. She watched in amazement as the mist expanded and morphed, changing its size and shape before vanishing.

Encounters with interdimensional beings during waking hours also became a common occurrence. One afternoon, Joey was looking out of our big living room window at the area between the two walnut trees, a section of our property that always held a strong pull and fascination for him. As he looked out the window, he saw a bearlike creature walking on all fours along the gravel road that passed our house. As it lumbered along, he watched as the back end began to morph, elongating until it looked like the legs of a panther. It then began to get an almost shimmer to it as it began to dissolve, vanishing as it passed the space between the two walnut trees. Just after that moment, Joey found himself in a trance state, which produced a vision. Tonya, her hair completely silver-grey, was sitting at the edge of a fountain in a large hall. People were coming up to her one by one to shake her hand. They would be spending the week with us, at what was a spiritual retreat and healing center. Meeting Tonya at the start of the week was something to which everyone looked forward.

Although Joey has been sharing this experience and vision for the past nine years, it was not until recently, as he was going through his dream and spiritual journals from 2003, that he remembered that he had had the same vision while lucid dreaming in the Brick Township apartment eight years earlier.

We have been working toward the manifestation of this vision ever since. In 2014, we opened an arts and education center that had weekly spiritual groups. We called it New Mystics, which was also the name of our theatre company and the art and literature website we founded in 2002. Joey believes that until Tonya lets her hair go silver-grey the vision as he saw it will not come to be.

That won't be anytime soon.

On another afternoon, Joey was driving up to our mailbox, about three quarters of a mile away from the house. As he approached the bank of mailboxes, Joey observed a gargoyle-like creature crouching by the side of the road as he exited the holler. The creature strongly resembled the protagonist in Joey's second novel, *Minor Confessions of an Angel Falling Upward*. The character, Planner Forthright, is a fallen angel with shape-shifting abilities. Joey had sent the manuscript to the publisher earlier that day. It seemed that Planner, who has sometimes attained almost a *tulpa*-like presence in our lives since he "showed up" in a poem in 2003, was acknowledging the accomplishment.

As is often the case, locations (and people) that experience high volumes of paranormal activity, as we do, often experience a wide range of phenomena, and our experiences at the holler house were no different. On several occasions, Tonya observed large orbs of light high in the sky over the holler. The orbs would pulsate and change colors while moving slowly up and down and side to side. In retrospect, Tonya has to wonder if these orbs resembled or were related to the objects that her grandmother observed over Van Buren, Arkansas thirty-six years prior.

Tonya also witnessed a UFO one December evening in 2014. She was lying in bed facing the window watching the snow falling when she noticed a flashing red light above the tree line near the top of the road leading out of the holler. At first she thought it was a radio tower, but she knew there was no radio tower located there. As she watched the light, it began to move below the trees, then rise above them, and then from side to side. Tonya ran to get her keys so that she could drive up the road to get a closer look, but by the time she got to the front door, the light was gone.

There were several other nights after this experience that Tonya saw unexplained lights in the sky that would move in a similar fashion, up and down and side to side.

Activity continued in cycles for the seven years we lived in our holler. A number of other spirits besides the little girl made themselves known to us. Jolie began to have dream visitations from spirits as well, and would often be jolted awake by having her hair or blankets pulled. Paranormal investigators provided independent corroboration while visiting our property that what we were seeing was real.

So did a Shawnee tribal chief. Details on that soon.

During our last three years in the holler, we had increasing experiences with beings referred to in Native American lore as "little people." We would see shadows of the diminutive beings scurrying around our living room. One about a foot high also ran across our bed as we lay in it one afternoon. Among indigenous tribes there are variations regarding what the little people's mannerisms are like; some depict them as benevolent while others describe them as evil. One belief, however, is common, and that is the understanding that the "little people" are a playful species of tricksters.

Sometimes, as with hauntings, it's all in your interpretation and mindset.

Our experiences with the "little people" bore out their playful, trickster nature. They seemed to have an affinity for shiny objects, which would often disappear and then reappear later in another location. One example of this happened on a sunny afternoon. Joey had retrieved a handful of coins from his pants pocket while standing in the living room. As he did so, a quarter fell from his hand, bounced up from the carpet, and vanished in midair. We searched every inch of the living room, pulling sofa cushions, lifting chairs, but the coin was nowhere to be found. About a week later, we found the coin in the middle of the living room floor. The location was obvious and there was no possibility that we had overlooked it for a week.

By this time we were years into our shamanic and Native American studies and had several friends from both the Shawnee and Lakota peoples. When a Shawnee chief came to our house to visit, he immediately noticed two things. The first was that he pointed out the exact spot in the living room where the "little people" typically gathered. We had not mentioned them to him. In the middle of a conversation, he simply pointed and said, "The little people like to gather there." The second was that, a year before, out of nowhere, six sycamores began growing around our property where we had accepted the offer to build a Lakota sweat lodge about a year before. Without a water source, the sycamores should not have been there. He told us they were there because the sweat lodge was. The Shawnee would look for sycamores for their settlements and holy sites because they knew water would be nearby. In this case, the Shawnee were acknowledging the holy site we had created.

This was interesting, and made a lot of sense with what had been happening prior to his visit. When we first began to do Lakota rituals within the sweat lodge and on the property around it, we saw a steep increase in the paranormal activity within and around the house. Lakota sweat lodge rituals are powerful in and of themselves. Many unexplainable things happen in the darkness of the lodge as the participants sing traditional songs in the Lakota language, steam is made by pouring water on heated river rocks, a ceremonial pipe is smoked, and spirits are beseeched and welcomed through prayer. What was surprising was that we could tell that the land and the spirits on it were also in an agitated state that did not seem logical given the intent and practices of the sweat lodge ceremonies.

During one of her many investigations of our property, Rosemary Ellen Guiley asked a simple question that quickly unlocked the mystery: "Are you honoring all of the tribal spirits who passed through this land, or just honoring the Lakota spirits, whose people never even settled here?"

We did some research right away because our answer was the Lakota spirits only. From that time on, we began naming all of the tribes with ties to that geographic area, especially the Shawnee, whose rituals and songs Joey began to incorporate, and the agitated energy disappeared. That is also when the sycamore trees began to grow.

Although encounters with the paranormal became an almost daily experience for us during our seven years in the holler, we never felt fearful or threatened, the way we did in the Tinton Falls house. Although, because of the frequency of the phenomena, we could label it *infestation*, it never felt dark and dangerous, and there was never any *oppression*. Rather, we came to welcome the experiences as an opportunity to explore and cultivate our abilities as paranormal investigators and as spiritual practitioners. By the time we sold the house to move on to our next adventure we had become so accustomed to unusual occurrences that we were very matter-of-fact about them and better able to process the things to come during our next two moves.

As we said earlier, some houses do not want you to move in, and some will not let you go.

It took us nearly two years to sell our dream home in the holler. The reasons we were selling were the same ones that made it hard to sell. It was a lot of property to upkeep, on a steep hill. It was isolated. The winters were treacherous because of the road. During one particularly bad winter, while Tonya was studying for her massage license in Pittsburgh (about an hour away) she did not come home for several weeks and our homeschooled daughter and Joey did not go out of the holler for six weeks.

After that winter, we decided to sell.

Feeling like our life was on hold for much longer than we wanted, we tried several real estate agents, all with the same outcome. The house would not sell. Some folks loved it, but there was always something blocking the sale.

Then we realized… it was something we had done with the property!

Right before the builders broke ground, we visited the property and did a ceremony where we placed a stone at each of the four corners of the land and asked the spirits to allow us to keep the property and all of us safe for as long as we were responsible custodians of it.

Having remembered what we did seven years earlier, we did a ceremony releasing the property.

It sold to an amazing family six days later.

Some houses hold you—sometimes not by your design. You will see what we mean when you read the section about our comfy and very active cottage in Leavittsburg, Ohio.

First, though, we share three years of consistent paranormal activity on the Crystal Coast of North Carolina.

Beaufort, North Carolina

There is an 85-mile stretch of North Carolina coastline known for its profound beauty and sparkling beaches. Tonya and Jolie fell in love with this stretch of Heaven, aptly called the Crystal Coast, also referred to as the Southern Outer Banks (and, as Joey was intrigued to hear, the Graveyard of the Atlantic), when they had the opportunity to join friends on their two-week vacation in the summer of 2012. Upon their return, Tonya had acquired a new goal—to relocate the family to a charming little town on the Crystal Coast called Beaufort.

Either the third- or fifth-oldest town in North Carolina, depending on which historian you ask, Beaufort has a rich maritime history, dating back three-hundred years to the time of Blackbeard and the Golden Age of Piracy. With its amazing waterfront views, historic homes, and quaint waterfront shops, it is no wonder Beaufort was named America's Coolest Small Town by *Budget Travel Magazine* in 2012 and by *USA Today* in 2020. Beaufort has also made other major magazine Top Ten lists in one way or another for nearly a decade.

In the summer of 2015, after (finally) selling our house in the holler and spending a paranormally quiet year in a two-bedroom apartment, we moved to a charming three-story townhouse, just two blocks from the waterfront in America's Coolest Small Town. Prior to moving there, we had heard that Beaufort is filled with ghosts, which is not surprising considering its age and colorful history.

As if the spirits, ghosts, and other entities were waiting for us to arrive, we began experiencing paranormal activity almost immediately after moving in.

Our townhouse was located directly across from the historic train depot, a Spanish Colonial Revival building with a steep roof covered in curved red tile. The depot, located at the corner of Broad and Pollock Streets, was active from 1907 until 1938, when train service ceased. The historic building currently functions as an annex to the Beaufort Town Hall and various groups use it for town and community meetings, as well as special events. One afternoon while doing the dishes, Joey looked out the second-story windows and saw a phantom train moving slowly down the street. The image of the train, while quite vivid, lasted only a moment and then vanished.

Shortly after moving in, Jolie began seeing the ghostly face of a man peering from around the corner of the wall that connected the living room and kitchen. For obvious reasons, she began referring to him as the "peeking man." This tactic, which is actually common, is referred to in the field as a "peek-around." It is most often associated with intelligent hauntings.

The third-floor hallway was also very active, particularly the area just outside of Jolie's bedroom door. The doorknob to her bedroom would often jiggle and on several nights Jolie would wake to the sound of a woman's voice softly talking on the other side of the door.

As we got to know our neighbors, whose townhouse shared a wall with ours, we learned that they were experiencing strange occurrences as well. We became better acquainted with these neighbors over time, as they owned and operated the health food stored located directly across the street from our townhomes where we frequently shopped. The couple had recently purchased the store and would take turns staying in the townhouse every other week while their spouse looked after their original store, located a few hours away. They were hearing footsteps and having doors close, but what startled them the most was when they observed a rocking chair in their upstairs bedroom begin rocking on its own. This activity, coupled with a feeling of someone watching them, became so disturbing to the wife that she stopped coming to Beaufort to stay at the house and left the running of the health food store to her husband.

We wondered about there being so much activity in a building that was only a few years old, so Joey did some research about the plot on which the townhouses were built. He learned that, prior to construction of the townhomes, there had been a building on the property that had served as military housing after World War II.

Tonya would frequently see ghosts in our bedroom. On one occasion, she was visited by a young woman whom she immediately knew to be from the Old Burying Ground—so named because it has churches on three sides—which was located just two blocks from our home. The woman projected an image of the monument marking her grave onto Tonya's mind's eye. The monument of a veiled young woman with her arms crossed over her chest was one that Tonya had not previously noticed during her strolls through the historic burial grounds.

The Old Burying Ground, which dates back to the early 1700s, is a hotbed of paranormal activity. Surrounded by wrought iron fences and shaded by canopies of ancient live oaks, the Old Burying Ground sits in the heart of Historic Beaufort. It was common when walking past the Old Burying Ground to hear disembodied footsteps following close behind us. When you stopped and looked, they stopped, and when you started walking, so did they. On several occasions, the footsteps followed us all the way home.

The next day, Tonya explored the grounds until she located the statue of the veiled young woman at the gravesite of Martha Washington Ramsey, 1846–1864 [see photo]. Tonya also discovered some information about the woman in a book we had purchased about the site, titled *Beaufort's Old Burying Ground: North Carolina*, by Diane Hardy and Marilyn Collins. According to the authors, Martha (or Mattie), was one of the many victims of the yellow fever epidemic that ravaged the area in 1864. Because Mattie had not given Tonya a specific message, other than to show her the monument, Tonya felt that she simply wanted to be noticed and remembered.

This is an important point to keep in mind if you experience a haunting. In horror films, the ghosts always want justice done or to reveal some terrible secret. But more times than not, ghosts simply want to be recognized. Just the act of acknowledging them will often be enough to end the haunting.

Another experience in the Old Burying Ground happened when Jolie decided to investigate the site with a friend who was a paranormal enthusiast eager to explore a genuine haunted site with his collection of investigative equipment. As they walked home afterward, they became aware of something casting a long, broad shadow on the sidewalk in front of them, as if a very large person was walking behind them. Jolie and her friend also heard the sound of heavy, booted footsteps following behind them and when they turned to look, no one was there.

Remember—when you investigate the paranormal, it also investigates you.

Although the Old Burying Ground is full of paranormal activity, the ghosts of Beaufort are certainly not contained within the boundaries of the wrought iron fences surrounding that site. Jolie and Tonya would see apparitions on the streets and in the windows of many historic homes and buildings during the day as well as every night.

In fact, Beaufort is so famously haunted that tourists travel from all over the world to participate in the Beaufort Ghost Walk, a ninety-minute tour of the town conducted by Port City Tour Company. Not long after we landed in Beaufort, Port City asked Joey to create a historical tour and educational content, including a special pirate-themed walking tour that he led on the streets of Beaufort for a year before being invited to conduct it on the grounds of the Beaufort Historic Site, a collection of buildings that includes the apothecary shop, schoolhouse, and jail.

One of the first spirits noticed by Tonya and Jolie in our townhouse was the ghost of a small boy about eight or nine years old. They frequently saw him playing at the top of the staircase or the entrance to the kitchen. Tonya began leaving toys in those areas for the boy to play with and when she would check on them the next day, he had moved them. The boy would also appear in the living room while we were watching television in the evening. He seemed especially drawn to Jolie. She would often feel him tugging at her ankles as she reclined on our chaise lounge, her favorite piece of living room furniture. One evening while Tonya was away, Joey was sitting with Jolie on the sofa watching television and he felt the quilt on his lap being tugged.

The peeking man made his identity known to Jolie after a period of several months, when he finally let her see him clearly one night when she was home alone. On that evening, Joey was leading a walking tour and Tonya was staying in a hotel in Mt. Airy, also in North Carolina (and the model for Andy Griffith's Mayberry) on her way to West Virginia. Tonya had called Jolie to check in for the night, and as they were talking, Jolie began to see the man peeking into the living room where she was sitting. She asked Tonya to hang up and check in at the townhouse psychically, to see if she could see the man and get a sense of him.

Tonya was immediately able to see the man. He was in his twenties, handsome and dark haired and dressed in what looked like a World War II–era military uniform. Tonya decided to do an Internet search for images of soldiers from the 1940s to see if she could find one resembling the man she was seeing. She asked Jolie to do the same so they could compare images and confirm that they were both seeing the same individual. After they each found images resembling the man they were seeing, they sent the images to each other. Although they did not pick the same photo, they had each selected images of young men with strikingly similar features. As she was looking at the image, Jolie kept psychically hearing the name William.

Over time, Jolie managed to make a connection with William and he became less timid. He stopped peeking at her from around corners, and would appear to her frequently, usually in her bedroom, although he would also accompany her to locations outside of our home. After several months of developing a strong connection to William, Jolie started to notice the presence of another spirit in her bedroom. The spirit of a barefoot, teenage boy dressed in jeans rolled at the cuffs and an old style tank top appeared in Jolie's bathroom one afternoon as she was taking a shower.

She quickly scolded him for brashly invading her privacy. Hearing Jolie sternly warn spirits to leave her alone became a common occurrence during our three years in Beaufort. By this point, William had become a protective presence for Jolie and he was not going to allow a "peeping tom" in her bathroom. Jolie watched as William forced the boy into her closet, where he remained for several months. During this time, Jolie began talking to the boy, assuring him that, while she had no problem with his presence, invading her privacy in the bathroom was not acceptable. We had taught Jolie the importance of establishing strong boundaries with the spirits and ghosts she was encountering and it was good to see her applying what she had learned with success.

As the father of a teenage girl, Joey found it ironic that, even though Jolie had no interest in dating, there were the ghosts of two young men—one a military veteran—taking up residence in her bedroom.

The boy in the jeans told her his name was Albert. He also told her that William would not permit him to leave the closet. Then, after many months of confinement, it appeared that Albert had gained William's trust, as Jolie began noticing him in her bedroom and in other areas of the house.

Another strange event occurred in the townhouse that Tonya had never experienced before, nor has she experienced it since. She had awakened in the middle of the night feeling quite thirsty, so she went to the kitchen for some water. As she stood in the kitchen quenching her thirst, she observed a woman sitting on the living room sofa. Unlike the impressions of ghosts and spirits that Tonya receives in her mind when she normally encounters them, the image of this woman had no intelligent energy emitting from it. In fact, it felt more like a projection than a spirit. While this was certainly strange, what Tonya really found odd was the woman's appearance. Her face was overdone with makeup, almost like a clown's, with caked white powder, too much blue eye shadow, and smeared red lipstick. More unsettling than the makeup, however, was the woman's expression. She sat there staring straight ahead with an over-exaggerated, maniacal grin on her face.

The next morning, Tonya mentioned what she had seen to our son. When she described the woman, he said, "Jolie and I watched *The Evil Dead* last night. There is a character in the movie named Linda, who looks exactly like that."

Tonya's theory is that the energy of the movie, and particularly the character, was so intense that it left an energy imprint on the living room. Fortunately, after that morning, Tonya never again saw the imprint of Linda in the townhouse.

This experience calls to mind another way you can protect your home from unwanted entities—by being aware of what you watch and listen to and how it effects both your energy and the energy of your home. As you will see in a case we investigated in Ohio, too much horror or paranormal material in your diet can cause an uptick in activity—and not the positive kind you may want.

We had been in Beaufort for almost a year when we had the opportunity to begin investigating a haunted library located in the neighboring town of Morehead City. We include a brief overview of our time at the library here; however, an in-depth account of our two-year, 150-hour investigation is available in our book *Watch Out for the Hallway: Our Two Year Investigation of the Most Haunted Library in North Carolina*. In May 2016, as Joey was preparing to lead a walking tour from the Port City storefront, he noticed a poster promoting a tour of the Haunted Webb Library. Intrigued, Joey inquired about how the tour worked. Before long, we were the new tour guides for the Webb Library, which we redesigned into an ongoing investigation that was open to the public.

The Webb Memorial Library and Civic Center is probably the most paranormally active place we have ever investigated. During our two years there, we encountered everything from classic haunting phenomena, such as flickering lights, doors opening and closing, footsteps, disembodied voices, and phantom music, to interdimensional beings, spectral Men in Black, ectoplasm, apporting objects, and wraiths and skeletal figures crawling along the ceilings.

We encountered resident ghosts, who were a fixed part of the phenomena at the Webb, and transient spirits who would pop in one night and be gone the next. One of the resident ghosts at the Webb was Dr. Sanford Thompson who was one of the two doctors who had offices in the building when it first opened in 1929. Our encounters with Dr. Thompson were always fun and enchanting, and definitely worth reading about in *Hallway*. Dr. Thompson, or Dr. T. as we affectionately came to call him, would frequently help us, as well as our guest investigators. He would provide messages, advice, and protection. And when we needed assistance crossing over lost souls, he was always there to help. Jolie would occasionally accompany us on our investigations, and when she did, William would follow her as a guardian and protector.

Our encounters with the transient spirits of the Webb were as varied as the types of phenomena that we experienced. One such encounter was with the ghost of a young man on fire, first seen by a boy of five when he was visiting the library one afternoon with his mother. As she was talking to the librarians at the circulation desk, the boy came running in from one of the back rooms. "Mommy!" he exclaimed, "There is a man on fire by the window!" Having experienced strange phenomena at the Webb in the past, the boy's mother ran with him back to the room where he had seen the burning man.

Although the woman did not see the man when she returned to the window with her young son, she knew that we were going to be investigating the Webb that evening, so she texted us an account of her son's sighting. Sure enough—that night we found the "man on fire" outside the library by the window, near to where the boy had reported seeing him.

It is important that we are not dismissive when children report such things. They are not as closed off energetically or as easily overwhelmed with sensory data as are adults and, as a result, they are more able to encounter such phenomena.

When we encountered the burning man, our electromagnetic frequency (EMF) meters were spiking red and there were some photographic anomalies—blurred shadows and unexplainable shafts of light. We attempted to cross him over, but he was afraid and unsure about what was beyond the light. Later that evening we tried again to cross him over. His presence according to the EMF meters was now weaker. Joey was thinking, "Go into the light" and from the P-SB11 we heard: "I think." The "man on fire," whose name, he finally told us, was Robert, followed us home that night at the invitation of William, who had come with Jolie and us to the Webb for the evening's investigation.

This is another important aspect of dealing with entities in your home or business. Not all of them are "stuck" in the place they are haunting. They are able to travel to other places just like the living.

In a dream, Jolie later learned that Dr. T., accompanied by a little boy ghost from the Webb that Tonya called Oliver because he reminded her of Oliver Twist, took Robert back to the Webb in the middle of the night. Dr. T. was unhappy that William had taken Robert to our house. Tonya had seen "Oliver" near the window looking at Robert during our investigation that night. Robert was back at the Webb when we returned the next evening, still unwilling or unable to cross over. Two weeks later, however, he was no longer there.

This single episode demonstrates that hauntings, and the various ghosts and spirits who create them, are complex in both their circumstances and their communications.

During our time on the Crystal Coast, residents and business owners frequently asked Tonya to visit their homes and businesses to help them understand or alleviate the paranormal activity they were experiencing and to share specifically who, or what, she was seeing or sensing there. One such location was a historic building in Beaufort that housed an art studio and massage therapist. Both of the occupants were experiencing an intense feeling of someone watching them, as well as classic haunting phenomena, such as footsteps, doors closing, and lights flickering. Tonya, honored to have been asked to assist and excited as well to get a tour of the beautiful historic building, which was originally a funeral home and residence for its director, fulfilled their request the first chance she had.

The building was just a few blocks from our home, and it was a gorgeous sunny afternoon, so Tonya decided to walk. She arrived a little early and took the opportunity to sit on the wrap-around porch and take in the flowers while she waited for the owner of the art studio to arrive and show her around. As she waited, the spirit of an elderly woman appeared on the porch. The woman had a friendly smile and childlike energy. She excitedly gestured toward the flowers, and showed Tonya an image of her watering and caring for them. Tonya got the distinct impression that the woman had lived in the house as a child and young adult, and that she had been quite proud of her flower garden. She then "took" Tonya inside the house by implanting images of its rooms and hallways in her mind's eye. Although Tonya had never been in the building before, she was able to see the interior as vividly as if she were actually inside.

The woman, who had indicated to Tonya that her name began with an "H" (perhaps Harriet or Henrietta), showed her the activity that was occurring on the first floor—items being moved, disembodied footsteps, and a sense of being watched. The woman then showed Tonya a man in the upstairs hallway. The man was dressed like an undertaker, all in black, and had a very serious demeanor. Tonya received the name "Frank" and saw him walking back and forth in the hallway, staring and creating an overwhelming sense of being watched. It was about this time that Tonya heard the owner of the art studio pull up, so she walked around to the side of the porch to meet her. She apologized for keeping Tonya waiting, but Tonya shared that it worked out great, as a spirit attached to the property had already been giving her a "virtual" tour of the building!

Tonya described her encounter with the friendly old woman and was not only able to share about the flowers, but the exact floor plan and location of experiences without the owner having to tell her anything about them. The owner was thrilled and amazed. She felt that the woman was probably the daughter of the man who ran the funeral home and was so glad to hear that she was still at home and happy. When Tonya shared what she had experienced with "Frank" on the second floor, the owner of the studio indicated that that was exactly the type of phenomena that she and the massage therapist who rented space from her on the second floor had been experiencing.

Joey was able to corroborate some of this information through his experience as creative director of Port City Tour Company. This building was one of the first stops on the Beaufort Ghost Walk. It was one of the attractions not only because it was a former funeral home, but because there had formerly been a hair salon there that had to leave because the owner would come in each morning to find that shampoo bottles and tubes of hair care products had been dumped out or sprayed all over the room.

On the day of her investigation, the owner of the building took Tonya inside and gave her an extensive tour of its beautiful restoration. When they got to the second floor, Tonya was able to have a conversation with Frank and asked him to please not stand behind and stare so intensely at the women, as it made them feel uncomfortable—so much so that both women tried to make a point of not being alone upstairs after dark.

Several weeks later, the owner of the art studio shared that, while they still felt his presence, the sensations of being intensely stared at had somewhat diminished and that they did not feel as creeped out when alone upstairs after dark.

As you can see, setting boundaries and explaining why you are setting them to the entities in your living or work space can go a long way toward decreasing activity to a comfortable level.

In honor of the ghost and her garden of flowers, the Beaufort Ghost Walk added this information to the tour, encouraging the guests to say hello to "H" and acknowledge her beautiful flowers.

Not everything paranormal has to be dark and violent. We have a responsibility to point this out whenever we can.

Tonya also had the opportunity to explore one of the many historic bed and breakfasts in Beaufort. All of Beaufort's bed and breakfasts are beautiful, but there is one in particular to which Tonya was especially drawn. It was only a few blocks from our house, so one day Tonya decided to walk over and ask the innkeepers for some information. The husband, who was finishing up with some guests, greeted her and asked if she could wait in the sitting room. Tonya was happy to wait, as she figured it was a perfect opportunity to tune in and see if there were any ghosts present. It did not take long for her to have an answer.

Within a few moments, Tonya saw the ghost of a little girl dressed in clothing that looked to be from the late nineteenth or early twentieth centuries. The girl had blonde ringlets and was probably around nine or ten years old. She waved at Tonya and Tonya waved back. She then proceeded to show Tonya some of her favorite activities by projecting images into Tonya's mind's eye. Through this mini-movie, the little girl shared that she loved playing games with the innkeepers, particularly in the dining room. She giggled as she showed herself moving silverware and other table items. She also showed lights flickering, as well as sharing the sound of footsteps on the stairs and in the hallway.

Before long, the innkeeper returned and was ready to answer Tonya's questions. He was kind enough to share some of the history of the inn, built in 1866. He shared some stories about the original family and showed Tonya a photograph of them that was hanging in the foyer. Among the faces, Tonya instantly recognized the little girl from the sitting room!

A few weeks later, after a business event at a local restaurant, we had the opportunity to spend some time with the innkeepers. The wife expressed her frustration that something was causing appliances and electronics to fail. We were able to offer her some strategies for appeasing the entities who were causing the damage and costing them a considerable amount of money.

A friend asked Tonya to visit her home in Morehead City. The woman and her family had been experiencing some activity and she had been experiencing difficulty sleeping, including bouts of sleep paralysis. Tonya noticed the spirit of a little girl wearing a sundress playing in the front yard. The little girl was quite friendly, and showed Tonya that playing in the yard had been one of her favorite activities. Tonya did a walk-through of the house and was especially interested in seeing her friend's bedroom, hoping she could find the underlying cause of what was keeping her from sleeping. Upon entering the bedroom, Tonya felt an energy portal in the area of the bed. She also noticed that there were two very large mirrors facing the bed. Reflective surfaces such as windows and mirrors can serve as portals to other dimensions and Tonya immediately felt that the mirrors were the culprits. She could sense that entities were entering into her friend's bedroom through the mirrors at night and feeding on her friend's energies.

Tonya recommended that her friend place blankets over the mirrors at night to prevent the flowing in of energies from other dimensions. She followed up with her friend a few days later and was happy to hear that since she had been covering the mirrors, she was sleeping much better.

If you are seeing an uptick of activity in your home, first check the location of mirrors, especially in the bedrooms and any rooms where the occupants spend a lot of time. We are seeing a substantial increase in entities entering through mirrors—including the dark, dangerous entity called the Hat Man—and we keep the mirror in our bedroom covered whenever we are not using it.

Our three years on the Crystal Coast were some of our most enjoyable. We count our blessings in having the opportunity to meet and work with many wonderful people. We also had the opportunity to help several people understand the experiences they were having in their homes, as well as to help them learn to tune into their own intuitive abilities.

We had the chance to live in a charming, historic, and haunted town while living in a new, but haunted, townhouse. In addition to our resident spirits—William, Albert, and the little boy (whose name we never learned)—we also had engagement with half a dozen other spirits, a few of whom had followed us home from the Webb. One of them caused some trouble in our kitchen for a few days, knocking an egg off the counter, spilling the milk in the refrigerator, and putting a plastic bread tie in the oven.

These spirits were of a transient nature and would simply come and go, but while they visited they made themselves known through knocking, footsteps, flickering lights, jiggling door handles, sharing impressions of their gravesites, and other phenomena.

As long as we declared our boundaries and kept our energy positive, these never escalated into anything more than interesting, enjoyable experiences.

Leavittsburg, Ohio

In April 2018, Tonya heard about the rental availability of a quaint Sears catalog cottage built in the late 1920s. The wood floors, fireplace, glass-faced wooden cabinets, and overall layout were ideal for our wants and needs and we secured it two months early so no one else would snatch it up while we were finishing our lease in North Carolina.

We knew before we moved in that there were active ghosts and spirits in this house, including a little boy in an upstairs bedroom walk-in closet and a man in the basement. A few days after Tonya first visited and saw the little boy, she received a "photo memory" notification on her phone, something that had never happened before. It was of the closet where the little boy lives, as if to say, "Hey, don't forget I'm here!"

She did not and he continued to appear to her, although with less frequency, as time went on. He would rustle the sheets at the foot of the bed at night to let Tonya know he was there.

We had been living in the house for a few weeks when Jolie reported seeing a man next to her bed. In our bedroom, something had moved Joey's collection of Asian god and goddess figurines into a different configuration. Going into his sunroom office, something had moved a collection of figures from the CW show *Supernatural* as well. It was notable that both sets of figures had a spiritual/paranormal focus. This was an indication of things to come.

It was on this same day that we first started to hear thumping noises on the front porch. We also heard something moving and bumping items in the kitchen. We were quickly moving from *manifestation* to *infestation*. The kitchen and sunroom office, which shared a wall, would be the epicenter of the many kinds of phenomena we would encounter in our two years (and counting) here. The upstairs hallway was also very active, with doors opening and closing, floorboards creaking, footsteps, the sound of something dragging items up and down the hallway, and the light in that hallway always switching on and off. We would hear thumping almost nightly after we left a room.

By the middle of the following month, August, something had moved more figures (this time from *Dr. Who*, in the sci-fi realm) and pushed a wide-based figure of a Universal monster off a shelf.

September began with Jolie and Joey both hearing a woman's voice in the upstairs hallway. At the time, they both assumed it was Tonya, who was reading in the bedroom upstairs. When they entered the bedroom and saw Tonya sitting quietly on the bed, they were not so sure, so they asked about to whom she had been talking. Not only had Tonya *not* been talking, she had not heard the woman's voice, although it had sounded to Joey and Jolie as if it was coming from the hallway right outside the bedroom door. Several days later, Tonya also heard a woman's voice. She was upstairs making the bed one morning and clearly heard the soft sounds of a woman's voice coming from Jolie's bedroom. The voice continued for several minutes and Tonya finally had to open Jolie's bedroom door and look inside just to make sure Jolie was not inside. She wasn't. This would be a recurring phenomenon. We were never able to make out what it was she was saying. Joey actually saw her in a white gown at least half a dozen times, always on the lower half of the split staircase into the living room. One afternoon, shortly after Joey had seen her, Tonya saw a white mist in that spot.

Jolie and Tonya saw ghosts and apparitions in other rooms of the house as well, sometimes full-bodied, sometimes only a part of the body, such as feet. Jolie frequently reported seeing the full-bodied apparition of a woman in a full-length yellow dress dancing around the first floor of the house.

As with the townhouse in Beaufort, Tonya often left toys in the closet where she had seen the ghost of the young boy during her first viewing of the house. Unlike the toys left out in Beaufort, these toys never moved. However, to Jolie's frustration, collectible dolls, horses, and figures in her bedroom frequently moved and were touched. The boy apparently enjoyed these items more than the vintage Fisher Price toys left for him in the closet by Tonya.

As we continued to make the house a home and the humidity of the East Ohio summer gave way to the beautiful colors and cooler temperatures of fall, the excitement began to build around the publication of *Watch Out for the Hallway*. Joey went out on the front porch the day before our first shipment of books was due to arrive, and there was a small metal shamrock by the door. There was no explanation as to how it got there. We took it as a sign of good luck and much success for the book and our work and we have not been disappointed.

The following day, as scheduled, the first shipment of the book arrived and, from the moment we opened the box, the phenomena in our home started to increase in both frequency and variety. That morning, while brushing her teeth, Tonya heard the floorboards in the hallway creak as she watched the bathroom door close on its own.

That afternoon, as Joey left the porch to get the mail from the box by the street, he came upon two broken plastic game tiles pressed into the stones of the driveway. One said "DEAD END" and the other had the number 3 [see photo]. DEAD END sounded ominous and on one level this message was a warning about some obstacles we would face during our time here, especially when we began the process of relocating to take advantage of some new opportunities elsewhere. As we are completing this book, more than two years later, the meaning of these tiles has become clear. Especially the 3: it will be three years and not the planned two, before we move.

That night, Jolie heard three thumps in her room and then her pillow depressed, as if someone was laying their head on it, next to hers.

The next day, Joey heard disembodied footsteps coming up the stairs as he was standing in the hallway at the top of the staircase. Later that day, while in the kitchen, in a moment of clairaudience, he heard a disgruntled, disembodied voice say "asshole" as he walked past the refrigerator.

There were several occasions when we received text messages and phone calls from Jolie while we were out having dinner with friends. On such occasions, Jolie, who was normally not rattled much by the activity in the house, had become unnerved by the sound of a heavy bag being dragged or thick-heeled boots stomping up and down the hallway, just outside her door.

Loud footsteps, thumps, and disembodied voices continued. One night, our oldest son, who was living with us at the time, heard a very loud humming sound coming from just below his window at 11:30 pm. He went downstairs in search of the source and could find nothing that would explain it.

On another occasion, Joey entered our bedroom to find that something had moved our bed so it was on a fifteen-degree angle from the wall. A few weeks later he watched a table on the back porch move an inch to the left before his eyes.

We also experienced phenomena related to books appearing in the middle of the floor or something moving heavy boxes of books we kept in the basement. One morning, we found a cookie that we had left in its wrapper on the coffee table in front of the sofa when we went to bed the previous night unwrapped and under the sofa.

At least no one had taken a bite out of it.

Unfortunately, there was plenty of bad behavior. Sometimes things were not just moved but knocked over or considerably rearranged. Joey entered his sunroom office one morning to find half a dozen model cars turned on their roofs. He would also hear, through clairaudience or through the spirit box, male voices cursing at him and calling him names, as had happened in the kitchen weeks before. While preparing for an investigation, Joey had his equipment box open and accidentally turned on the P-SB11 spirit box. He immediately heard two male voices, one older, one younger, say:

"Lights? Christ! Jerk! She's coming." Tonya then entered the room and the communication stopped.

Although Tonya heard her name whispered by a man on another occasion, there was no cursing or insults aimed at her.

After many sessions with the spirit box, consulting with other psychic mediums, doing research on the house deed at the local library, and the synchronicity of receiving a painting done by the original owner, we learned that the ghost most upset with us and causing the bulk of the activity was a man named Frank. He did not like the technology of the modern age—and Joey's sunroom office, which was set up for audio and video recording and editing, was chock full of technology.

One day, Frank became unusually agitated—banging and moving things around—and Joey realized he had been verbally expressing his frustration with a client with the same name.

Frank ripped two Japanese fans off Jolie's wall and she heard him whisper, "I don't like things from Asia."

About a year after we moved in, as Joey spent more and more time in the library room because of Frank's increasing mischief in the sunroom, the activity began to ramp up in there. One night around 2 am—while Joey was away on a three-week tour—Tonya heard noises downstairs and had a feeling of foreboding. Entering the library, she felt like it was "alive"—she heard crackling noises all around her and the room looked like it was on an angle. The hairs on her neck and arms stood up. She slept with the light on for the next week.

It was not until sixteen months after we moved in, in October 2019, that Tonya at last saw Frank. From that night on, getting a sense that it would ease the tensions, she would leave him food and drink in the kitchen at dinnertime.

A month later, we invited another investigator to stay the night at the house. By this time, our children had moved out and we were less worried about increasing the activity by paying close attention to it and running the equipment.

We received many communications, from a man moaning in the living room to a "Hi" in the basement. Frank was at peace with our new arrangement, but there was evidence that other ghosts and spirits—including one that had lived in the house just before us and perhaps had died not long after—were using the house as a pass-through.

A good portion of the activity also had to do with the county's maximum-security prison sitting only half a mile from our home. On the weekend of the investigation with our colleague and on subsequent occasions when we ran a spirit box, we would get dozens of different men's names and words, such as *felon, inside, separate, murder, scare, shot,* and *building.* We also knew from a separate case we had worked on—related in Part II—and further research we had done that violence, including murder, was part of life among the staff and inmates there.

One day, in the middle of the winter of 2020, with several inches of snow on the ground, Joey, going a little stir crazy in the house, bundled up and went outside to walk the property and do a tobacco ceremony. He chose the back property line, where a beaded and buckskinned Native American male had shown himself to Tonya on several occasions prior. We felt that he was a guardian spirit for us against the energies of the prison and Joey wanted to thank him, as things had been relatively quiet. As Joey was doing the ceremony his intestines started to cramp and he began dry heaving, which is consistent with when he is around elevated amounts of EMF. About five months later, Tonya saw the Native American. She offered him tobacco and then watched him morph into a furry creature with large ears and eyes that was definitely not of this world.

In mid-May 2020, we began to notice activity ramping up in the kitchen again. We knew it was not Frank (we thought he had passed on and received confirmation two months later). The ghost was very friendly in its energy. After about a week of Tonya seeing him there each night, she was readying the coffee before bed one evening when she heard a friendly "Hello!" She also started hearing REM's "Great Beyond" every time she entered the kitchen.

The next day, we turned on three different devices for contacting spirits with the aim of finding out who it was. On the first, as Joey began to ask questions, we got the message, "Slowly." Then: "Light lovely." The first was in answer to Joey asking too many questions without pausing for an answer and the second we took as a commentary on life on the Other Side. We had a thought about who it was. When we got no further answer, we switched to a second device. We immediately heard, "I am David." This was exactly who we thought it was—a former board member of our nonprofit who also set up our arts center according to the principles of *feng shui*. He was also Tonya's Reiki Master Teacher. David had passed suddenly from a heart attack a few months earlier. A week prior to his appearing in our kitchen, we had been burning some old papers from the nonprofit in our fire pit and some of the papers pertained to him. We decided to continue the fire in his honor, adding flat cedar and some sage to it to thank him for all he had done for us. We had burned up papers and dedicated the fire to him again just a day before he appeared in the kitchen. On a third device, Tonya asked him to confirm that it was our friend and he said, "Yes ma'am." We then asked if we could relay the message to his wife. He said, "Sure!" We started by asking her if David was an REM fan, to which she responded with an enthusiast "Yes he was!" After we relayed the messages, she told us she was going to play "Great Beyond" at his upcoming memorial service.

These are the best days for us when it comes to the paranormal.

Nonhuman Entities

Not everything encountered in the "Creative Cottage," as we came to call it, was human. Jolie witnessed a brownish blob by the lower half of the split staircase where Joey would see the woman in white. She also saw and sketched a creature with the head of a girl and the body of a spider [see sketch]. This creature also appeared in the home of a colleague of Tonya's, to both the woman and her boyfriend. It is possible that it was something that latched onto both of them in a spiritual center where they both freelanced where there was a variety of phenomena, some of which was dark.

Joey was psychically attacked one night while working on a screenplay, a paranormal thriller based on a true story that always seemed to invite strange phenomena around those associated with it (similar to the experiences that some of the guest investigators involved with our Webb investigation had after they received the book). He felt a sharp pain in his back and an oppressiveness in the air. Tonya was out so he consulted a colleague who is a psychic and she suggested going outside and holding onto a tree. He chose the hawthorn tree in front of the house that is the center of faerie activity on the property. Within seconds, he felt the pain and oppression release and watched a black mass, well over six feet tall, leave him and cross the street. As it did so, Tonya pulled into the driveway and drove right past him. Joey was not even aware it happened, although it was evening, the headlights were on, and the car passed only six feet from the tree. He was surprised when he walked toward the house and saw her car.

On another evening, about ten months after we moved in, Joey saw a black mass come out of the wall toward him in their bedroom. It was also around this time that he began having nightmares every few weeks, at times causing him to wake up or have Tonya wake him up because he was shouting in fear. In one of those dreams, a malevolent entity lifted him up while he was investigating a basement and he yelled out and woke up as his back was being broken on a pipe with a red valve protruding from it that ran along a beam in the ceiling.

Over a year later, while watching a documentary about a house with a dark, dangerous entity inhabiting it, Joey was astonished to see the *exact* basement from that dream!

Things were reasonably quiet for most of winter 2020. Tonya was away for work a lot and Joey settled into a quiet routine of editing, writing, and reading. That all changed when we received an email in April 2020 from a close friend who was seeing an uptick of activity in his home. Much of it was poltergeist activity—something kept opening a drawer in a bedroom chest. Our friend put industrial-sized rubber bands on the handles to keep it from opening. He awoke the next morning to find the rubber bands snapped and the drawer once again open. The next day, after reporting that he felt like something was watching him, he found the door from his house to the garage and the door from the garage to the outside both open.

We sent him some strategies for how to cleanse and ward the house and we did several meditations to help clear the space. Although it worked, we then had activity in our own home, including having a window in our bedroom (that we know was locked) opened by an unseen force.

A few weeks later, we were on a late night radio show that finished at 3 am, the "hour of the wolf" or "witching hour." As we were talking about the show two days before on our weekly livestream program on the paranormal and spiritual, *Into the Outer Realms*, several listeners heard an animal-like growl, which is clear on the archived version of the show. During the radio program that evening, one of the people in the chatroom was posting about demonic entities and other dark things. We were both getting a bad feeling every time his messages appeared. As is typical with radio protocol, the host did not mention it and neither did we. After the show, as we got ready to sleep in our bedroom, we had a terrible feeling that something malevolent was watching us. Joey went downstairs to get something and the lights in the hallway outside our bedroom began to flicker. We burned palo santo, sage, and frankincense resin and warded our bed with crystals and religious objects. As we lay there in the dark, Joey saw in his mind's eye the outline of two winged creatures in the corner of the bedroom. We had a difficult time falling asleep that night. We say without embarrassment that we extremely frightened by that experience.

The "Mothman Effect"

In the 2002 Mark Pellington–directed film based on John Keel's *The Mothman Prophecies*, one of the two characters representing Keel (the other being Richard Gere's reporter, John Klein), Alexander Leek, says, "You noticed them and they noticed that you noticed." Although this has applied wherever we have lived and investigated—leading us to dub it the "Mothman Effect"—it was perhaps most pronounced in the spring and summer of 2020, when we did our weekly livestream show, *Into the Outer Realms*.

We always use the library for the broadcast, which, as of this writing in mid-September 2020, has become the home's hotspot, along with the rooms with which it shares walls—the bathroom, living room, and kitchen. The library is where our friend and mentor, Rosemary, visited Joey two days before she died in July 2019. We have mentioned other phenomena that occurred in the library in previous sections.

In early June, we were discussing Dr. Thompson, a benevolent spirit from the Webb Library, when the chandelier above our set began to flicker. Again, like with the growl, numerous audience members noticed it. Similar to the EMF meter going to red whenever Tonya would talk about the doctor in our first investigation of the Webb, the lights would flicker only after we mentioned him. After the show, we went into the living room and, turning on the chandelier over the couch, we saw that all of the bulbs were burned out.

In mid-June, we were Skyping with a colleague who is a psychic medium and he noticed a woman with black hair and a man with a Quaker hat behind us where we sat on the living room couch. He was confident that they were pass-throughs who meant us no harm.

On June 29, as Joey was working in the library, he saw a full-bodied apparition walk past the double glass doors between the living room and the library. The next day, the light and fan turned on in the bathroom, the door of which is in the library. On July 1, a few minutes after Tonya arrived home from a road trip, the faucet in the bathroom turned on while we were standing in the kitchen, about ten feet away.

On July 3, we did an episode of *Into the Outer Realms* about tools for guidance and protection. We had many powerful ritual objects in the library that we demonstrated or showed, including a Tibetan singing bowl, several stones and crystals, oracle and Tarot decks, and various herbs (e.g., sage and rosemary). During the broadcast, several psychic mediums in the audience were commenting in the chatroom about an energy vortex swirling around us, and several ghosts and spirits they could see. One was a woman dressed entirely in black. She was sending healing light to Joey's heart and nose (he had been having trouble with both at the time). During a meditation a few days later, the woman in black visited Tonya. In another example of the "Mothman Effect," Joey knew who she was after Tonya described her, in part because he had been researching his ancestry for months prior and had identified two of his four great-grandmothers as having psychic abilities of various kinds, and perhaps practicing the Italian form of wicca called *stregheria*. Exactly two weeks earlier, Joey's second cousin, having watched the show, messaged him to say that members of the family had referred to another of his great-grandmothers, named Palma, as a "mistress of the occult." Tonya was then able to verify her identity from a photo Joey showed her. Our talking about her must have led her to us. She gave some further advice to Tonya about Joey's health and has since stayed with us, offering further guidance and help.

Another spirit that the audience was seeing was a woman with burns on her face. Tonya was able to contact her a few days after and found out that she had died in a house fire in the 1970s near to where our house is. Tonya was able to cross her over.

There was also a female trickster spirit that, according to one of the psychic mediums in the audience, was intent on knocking off or moving something from the shelf behind us. She convinced the woman to wait until the show was over. Sure enough, within five minutes, a small sculpture of a raven was laid on its side (it has a wide base, so it could not have fallen over) and a model car (from the show *Supernatural*; remember the objects from that show that were moved in the sun room a year earlier?) had been moved. Having had her fun with us, the ghost went to the home of the psychic medium who "outed" her and caused enough trouble that she did a special ceremony to remove the ghost from her home. She managed to capture a photograph of her outside the kitchen window where she was doing her ceremony.

As to the man in the Quaker hat, all he said to Tonya was, "Enjoy the house."

The activity continued to increase for another few weeks and not all of it was pleasant and welcome. Tonya could see an older man smoking in our upstairs office and there were times we heard the office chair rolling around on the floor. There were knocks and bangs. Things were moved. We were encountering some dark entities that others corroborated as Tonya was having video sessions with her clients who were reporting oddly shaped black masses in one corner of the home, just behind our couch, similar to what guests had been seeing during our live broadcasts and the video dinner with the psychic medium.

A few hours after a video session where Tonya's client sent her photos and video of the black mass in the corner of the house, Joey was working in the library when he saw grey-white smoke rising up just beyond one of his laptops on the far side of the table. Tonya had seen it earlier in the day, which she only shared with Joey when he called her in to see if she was seeing the smoke as well.

Closing a Portal with Spiritual and Celestial Guidance

At this point, we knew it was time to call upon our spirit guides, especially Joey's aunt and great-grandmother and one of our mentors, all of whom were sticking close to us at this time. Using a pendulum and dowsing rods, we learned the following: there were three entities frequenting the space in addition to our trio of protectors. One was the old man, who meant us no harm. The other two were malevolent. One they did not give us much information on, other than that it was not human. The other was a collection of the negative energy of the area in which we were living (which is a rustbelt town with high poverty and drug addiction; many of the neighborhoods have empty or blighted commercial properties and homes). They also told us that the corner of the room where people were seeing the black mass was a portal and they gave us detailed instructions on how to close it. They also told us how it was originally opened: the faeries from the hawthorn tree used to dance in that area before the house was built. It was fairly large, encompassing both floors of the house. Our guides instructed us to pull everything out of the two rooms involved and do a thorough cleaning, after which we were to sage. On the first floor, they told us to place a mirror facing the corner of the room to keep the entities from coming in. It would remain there for a week. We decided to use a makeup mirror on a stand with three panels of mirrors that we could angle precisely into the corner. We fastened the mirror to a five-foot ladder after receiving confirmation that this was a good way to go.

They also suggested a series of steps that were later superseded by a blend of synchronicity and celestial intervention we will share a little later.

We planned to do the initial work in two days' time, on a Saturday. The day before, a client had asked Tonya to see her in person at her home that morning, and Joey decided to surprise her by getting most of the work of moving the furniture and setting up the ladder done before she returned.

What ensued was a ninety-minute "spiritual scavenger hunt" that resulted in a ceremonial fire, the collection of flat cedar, hawthorn branches and leaves, a blue jay feather, and an exchange of gifts of stones for heavy cream and a marble for the faeries. It was a wonderful reminder that trusting your intuition and your guides and being open to what they tell you can lead to memorable journeys and the management of difficult paranormal phenomena.

The following Friday we experienced unexplainable lights and shadows and odd knocking during *Into the Outer Realms*. At one point, Joey put his hand on Tonya's leg under the table because he thought she was nervous (we were recording the audio of the episode separately for later rebroadcast on KGRA Radio and also debuting a new multimedia opening for the show, which required some extra steps during the livestream). After some investigation, we were able to determine the source of the knocking. A woodpecker had been pecking away on the side of the house. We were not, however, able to find a mundane explanation for the lights and shadows.

That evening, as Joey was preparing his notes for the next part of the portal closing the following day, he received an email message from a man who claims to be a Celestial Being who is inhabiting a body on Earth to be with his wife, who had incarnated here thousands of years ago. He is able to maintain contact with his Celestial self on a spaceship related to Ashtar in a different dimension by essentially bilocating energetically. He offered to Joey a short mantra that he could use to contact the starman's space brothers and sisters. Tonya was engaged in a video meeting, so Joey went outside and tried to make contact, which resulted in streaks of light in the sky that he cannot explain away as aircraft or clouds. He and Tonya had seen these streaks of light after a communication from Celestial Beings through automatic writing at the start of the COVID-19 pandemic.

That night, he and Tonya decided to do a special guided meditation using Robert Monroe's hemi-synch gateway technique before going to bed to ask for more guidance on the second phase of closing the portal. Joey also used the mantra the Celestial Being gave him.

A group of beings in silver suits visited Tonya, closing the portal with a piece of technology. They also warded the house and property using purple light.

Checking in with our trio of guides, they confirmed that the Celestial Beings had indeed closed the portal and warded the house and property and that we did not need to do the rituals they had given us the week before.

The timing of the contact by the man claiming to be a Celestial Being gives credence to his claim, given the help provided to close the portal by his brothers and sisters from space and the confirmation from our guides. Joey continues to be in contact with him, as a learning experience on several levels.

A month later we invited some colleagues to the house, one of which had experienced various phenomena here ten months earlier. They reported encountering ghosts and spirits, male and female, including a male with a crew cut that one colleague saw standing in the sun room and the other saw standing in the library.

We feel compelled to repeat at this point that it is not ideal to be doing investigations in your home and, as we have said elsewhere, we keep them to a minimum. But, between writing and researching the paranormal for hours every week, being on our own show plus several others every month and talking to talented guests who are often demonstrating spiritual and other practices, our home in Leavittsburg is like a lighthouse on a foggy night at the seashore. And, as a result of this "Mothman Effect," the activity is almost constant, but—with the exception of a few harrowing experiences we have described—has been manageable and mostly pleasant.

An Unexpected Family Visitor

We have chosen to end this section on Leavittsburg with perhaps the most challenging formerly human roommate from beyond one could ever wind up sharing a space with: your mother or mother-in-law.

Exactly one month after we moved in, Tonya's mother suddenly passed away. Shortly after, we moved her father to a house about two blocks from our own. Without going into too much detail about family dynamics, it became apparent about a year later that Tonya's mother was unhappy with the amount of time and attention Tonya's father was getting from us. How did we know? Silverware from his house would appear in our silverware drawer! She was clearly saying, "Have him over for dinner more!" Then, as we were writing this book, a pair of toenail clippers appeared on the kitchen counter, directly above the silverware drawer. We each have our own pair, which we each accounted for, in the bathroom where they belonged. A few days prior, Tonya had seen her father clipping his toenails. If you think you know what comes next, so did we. Until she asked her dad about it. He said his *were* missing. BUT, *the ones found on our counter weren't his!*

It could be that something went wrong with the transfer. It is possible we will never know. And, if you should happen to need a pair of slightly haunted nail clippers, we have an extra set.

Although she was certainly giving us a hard time about the frequency of having Tonya's father over for dinner, we weren't exactly sure what she was trying to convey with the clippers. We also weren't the only ones she was sharing her "suggestions" with. Two months after she passed, Tonya got a reading from our friend and colleague from England, psychic medium Carole Bromley. Tonya's mother came through almost immediately to let Carole know that she had been trying to implore a man named "Collins" to stop tampering with the light at the top of our stairs. Carole shared with Tonya that her mother had been lecturing Collins that his behavior was very rude and needed to stop. After several weeks, the light at the top of stairs did indeed stop flickering.

Perhaps Tonya's mother was finally able to convince Collins to mind his manners and leave our lights alone.

Part II: From Our Case Files

Introduction

Before we share with you some of our most intriguing and challenging cases, we want to thank everyone who has trusted us enough to invite us into their homes and businesses to investigate and in many cases deal with a haunting. Our mentors taught us that charging money for an investigation is not something that an investigator should do, and we have always honored that advice. If we have traveled a long distance, we might receive travel money, a place to stay, or join them for a meal, but other than that, there is no *monetary* compensation when we take a case.

We italicized monetary because we do receive compensation in the sense of our clients allowing us to use the cases that we work on in our workshops, lectures, and books such as this. This experiential data are invaluable to the work that we do and we are deeply appreciative of the opportunity to share these stories with you, as there is nothing like real-life examples when it comes to education.

As you can imagine, and will better understand as you read the details of these cases, sharing people's real names, locations, and other identifying facts would make for an uncomfortable situation for everyone involved. With this in mind, we use pseudonyms, talk generally about the people involved, and otherwise change locations and other details in order to protect our clients.

That said, *all of the phenomena, the overall structure of the background information,* and *how the case unfolded are factual.* We have been very careful in this regard. All of the manifestation, infestation, and oppression we share in the pages to come happened as reported.

One final thing. As you will see, investigation of the paranormal can be dangerous, stressful work.

A colleague who investigated dark entities for many years confided that she had finally gotten rid of certain artifacts from her home and wanted to move from a place she very much loved because of what they had done to her. Another colleague was forced to abandon an investigation of a section of woods near his home that he owned when dark entities began planting violent suggestions related to his pets and family in his mind.

We always keep them in mind as we undertake a case.

A Tragic Case of Misidentification in Ohio

Every experience we have with the paranormal or supernatural has something valuable to teach us. Not only are no two cases the same—the variables are considerable. There is the site itself, which is acted upon by the architecture, the geography, the history of the people who lived there prior, the current residents, and of course the ghost(s), spirit(s), and other entities interacting there. There are also the circumstances and intensity of the haunting to consider, as well as what all parties concerned wish the ultimate outcome to be.

Not long after we had moved to Ohio, a wellness center where Tonya was working a few days a week referred us to a potential client. After a quick phone call and series of texts between Tonya and the prospective client, it was clear that something significant was going on in the home and we wanted to help the family sort it out.

During our initial visit to the home—a comfortable, cozy rental in a quiet, tree-lined neighborhood—we spent the first hour with the client and her boyfriend taking a case history and answering questions. The boyfriend was skeptical that the activity was paranormal but wanted to be supportive of his housemate and her two teenage daughters (who were not there that day or during a subsequent visit).

As the narrative unfolded while we sat at the kitchen table taking their history, it was clear that this was in many ways a classic case. First, there were missing items. The client had bought three protective stones and one had disappeared. The client had also started wearing a necklace with a protective stone, and she claimed she had felt it yanked off her neck. She also reported having her legs and feet touched while in bed. A bathroom brush had disappeared and reappeared twelve hours later. There was also poltergeist activity—the shower curtain had been pulled down (it had an adjustable rod but it was secure when we tested it) and towels had been pulled off a rack. This second incident in the bathroom made it harder to dismiss the shower curtain as having been a rod that became loose on its own.

We also knew from experience that bathrooms are very active areas. And, if you think about it, there is a clear difference between *pulled down* and *fell*.

The client went on to report odd noises, feelings of being watched, previous paranormal experiences in other places she lived, and a sense that what was supposed to be their dream home at the start of a new chapter in their lives was fast becoming a place of nightmares and lack of peace.

In technical terms, manifestation had moved to infestation and they were crossing into oppression.

As similar as the patterns were to other cases of hauntings, there were some unique features as well. The client was a big fan of the paranormal "reality" shows and it was clear that they had influenced how she was handling the haunting. Further complicating the situation was the client's history of trauma. Although she had made considerable strides toward healing over the years, her perception of the phenomena was clearly colored through the lens of her trauma, and because of this, Tonya knew that it would be necessary to work with the client to provide tools and strategies for managing her stress. This included some Reiki sessions to help to facilitate relaxation as well as to assist the client in grounding and balancing her energy body.

Making the situation worse was the fact that, prior to our being referred to her, she had consulted a professed psychic who had told her, after a *brief* phone conversation, that the house needed an exorcism and the client was to avoid being in the home by herself. The psychic also suggested a set of rituals that sounded more like something out of a horror movie rather than a professional investigation. Given this dramatic presentation and our client's familiarity with TV shows where mediums share unnecessarily scary and at times inappropriate information with families in crisis, we found ourselves in a situation that the dispensing of bad information and inaccurate remedies had escalated without a competent professional ever conducting a single hour's investigation.

Considering the fact that they had moved in right around Halloween and the activity had started to manifest almost right after, we could clearly see that we needed to prevent any additional ingredients from being added to this already complicated recipe for fear and high anxiety. That meant, before turning on a piece of equipment or touring the house room by room, we had to do our best to set the client's mind at ease while also reassuring her boyfriend that we believed, based on all we had thus far heard, that there was indeed a haunting.

It was clear from what they had reported that the ground floor hallway, which led to three bedrooms and a bathroom, was an active center for phenomena. Their dog would not enter the hallway and their two cats were sensitive to it. The client also reported footsteps heard from the hallway when no one was in the area. She said she had felt someone staring at her from the end of the hallway as well. She also claimed to have seen a figure sitting on her daughter's bed. The energy of whatever was haunting them was "dark," she said, and they were frightened of what it might do.

For these reasons, it was an easy decision to start the investigation in the hallway. Joey unpacked our equipment, explaining to the client and her boyfriend how he used each instrument, what it measured and how it collected data, and how it all contributed to a thorough investigation. He first set up on a tripod and turned on a digital video camera, which he aimed down the hallway with a laser grid attached just above the lens to alert us to any movement. He turned on the P-SB11 spirit box and activated a digital voice recorder, which he sat beside it. Last, he turned on an EMF meter and temperature gauge.

Although no activity was picked up by any of these instruments, a clear male voice saying "Help!" was picked up through the spirit box by the digital voice recorder.

Just because a spirit or ghost does not make itself known through most of the equipment doesn't mean there is nothing there. As much as we would like corroboration between the case history, the equipment, and what Tonya or other psychic mediums are picking up, it doesn't always happen. In this case, Tonya could clearly see a man in his late twenties or early thirties in the hallway. Knowing that she saw him, he entered one of the daughter's bedrooms (perhaps confirming the client's claim of having previously seen a figure in there) and out through the exterior wall. An instant later, Tonya could see him on the neighbor's roof.

Now we were seeing some corroboration. Around mid-January, a pair of special use, expensive shoes had disappeared from that bedroom. It had been several months and still they were missing. More seriously, the previous September, the teenage girl who lived in the house on whose roof the ghost now crouched had tried to commit suicide by taking a large dose of pills. This was a direct connection to the case because the daughter whose shoes had gone missing had recently had an out of character emotional breakdown where she said that she was worthless and not good enough.

As Tonya tried to communicate with the young man, she realized that he had committed suicide, with a handgun. So now we had a probable pattern of his depression and despair affecting the teenage girls. We did not believe then, nor do we now, that he was affecting them that way on purpose. It was the quality of his energy. We had experienced this during other investigations when a ghost had suffered a severe injury or radiated an intense emotion that the investigators felt when they stood within its energy field. There was clearly cognitive damage from the suicide that was causing him confusion and hampering his ability to communicate.

Increasingly confused and upset, the ghost then disappeared. By now it had been several hours and it was clear that the client and her boyfriend were suffering from data processing fatigue and we were not going to get any more information from them or the ghost on that day. We packed up and offered to come back again in a week. In the meantime, we advised them to stay away from the paranormal shows and to make an effort to let the ghost know that they wanted to help him if they could.

A few days later, we received a text from the client saying they had heard footsteps above the living room ceiling, a strange smell/foul odor had been following her around the house, and that one of the daughters, while working on a computer in the basement, had heard heavy breathing and a "huff" in her ear.

The client had also called a paranormal show, but they were more interested in *recording* the activity than helping to stop it.

When we returned several days later, we decided to set up the equipment in the basement based on the recent text and the initial case history. Since the haunting had begun, something had smashed a plaster snowman on the floor and had pushed a flowerpot off a shelf. Something had also knocked over the cat tree, which was a compelling piece of data because the client had reported that one of the cats had heard something in the living room one evening and had growled at it. Soon after, the cat had starting relieving itself on the bathroom floor instead of using the litter box in the basement. As you will read about in two of the cases that follow, cats are adept at sensing paranormal activity. At least in part, science tells us why. Cats spend most of their waking hours in an alpha brainwave state, at a frequency of 7.5 Hz. Alpha brainwaves are linked to transcendental meditation and psychic phenomena or intuition, which is why cats are incredibly sensitive to the paranormal and sometimes pay a very high price when malevolent ghosts or other entities become aware of them.

The basement had an access door to the garage, and one morning the client found herself locked out for twenty minutes or so on the basement side of it. The door to the garage would not open during that time, even though the locking mechanism was on the basement side of the door!

Recall the experience of our housemate in our home in Tinton Falls.

Not long after we had set up the equipment, Tonya saw the ghost in the basement. Although he could not manage any verbal communications, he did manage to answer Yes/No questions by making the temperature gauge on the P-SB11 increase, so that it flashed a red light and beeped. He also used the EMF meter to answer, by making it register in the red.

We soon had his name and the year that he had died. At that point, we used the Internet, especially Facebook, to gather further information, which we continued to use the spirit box red light/beeping and EMF meter to confirm. Tonya then found a photograph that matched the young man she was seeing.

What we learned was that his life had been a challenge, filled with opioid abuse and violence (his girlfriend, who had committed suicide a year after he did, had once attacked him with a knife). The house he was haunting previously belonged to his parents and, when things got too difficult for him to manage, he would stay in their basement, sometimes for several weeks.

Similarities between the client's boyfriend and the young man's father seemed to be causing additional confusion as to where the young man was. Both were musicians—guitar enthusiasts. The basement was filled with all kinds of musical instruments (the daughters played in their middle and high school bands) and recording equipment. Just enough similarity to make the young man wonder where his parents were and why these strangers were in their home.

Despite our best efforts to gain his trust, he would not answer any Yes/No questions about his suicide. He was getting frustrated, which was causing Joey's chest to tighten because of the intensity of his energy. We asked him if he wanted something. He indicated "Yes" but was unable to articulate what it was.

Tonya attempted to cross him into the Light, but he was not ready to go. Perhaps he was frightened of what was waiting for him there, or he was unable to process what it was.

Again realizing that his frustration and fear would not yield any further data, we packed up and stressed to the client that gentle communication with the ghost was what was needed and we would consult with our colleagues and figure out the next steps in our plan.

When we returned home, Joey reviewed the video footage. He saw a softball-sized orb of white light that move diagonally across the frame. Although there is always a possibility that it was dust, it moved diagonally down and then went back up toward the ceiling. It also coincided with our communications with the ghost.

Unfortunately, we had to make the difficult decision not to return to the house. The client contacted us by text within an hour of our departure claiming that the ghost was throwing rocks at her. In the days that followed, she claimed that it was not the ghost of a young man at all, but a demon pretending to be one so it could possess her. She was not following our advice, she was creating a great deal of fear for her family as well as for the ghost, and her inability to separate what she was actually experiencing from her past trauma made it clear that our involvement was not serving her best interests, nor those of her family. Tonya referred her to a mental health professional so that she could receive the help she needed in resolving her past trauma as a first step to calming the situation. However, to Tonya's disappointment, the client did not wish to seek out therapy.

Knowing there was no more we could do, we suggested that she find other investigators. We hoped that their independent investigation would corroborate our own and move the client toward a peaceful resolution.

The last we heard, she had had priests and other clergy come to the house to try to cleanse it and exorcise the young man from the home.

As professional investigators, it is of course important to listen to what your client is reporting with an open mind. However, it is also extremely important to factor in all the data and circumstances as they relate to the client. In this particular case, the client was becoming increasingly agitated, fearful, and at times even paranoid. The horror-film-like advice so casually given to her by the phone psychic had contributed to this. As a wellness professional, Tonya must always be sure that the services and advice that she offers are within her scope of practice, meaning that her actions and recommendations are limited to that which the law allows for the education and experience of the services she offers. Although there is no certification, licensing, or governing board for paranormal investigators, we must adhere to a strict code of ethics. We have made a start on this with our Paranormal Bill of Rights. Therefore, if a client is exhibiting behavior that is clearly outside of your experience and training to deal with—in other words, outside of your "scope of practice" as an investigator or psychic—the client must always be referred to the appropriate professionals.

A Dangerous Case in Pennsylvania

The Initial Interview

Every so often a case comes along that pulls in such a wide variety of phenomena that it presents challenges that require us to proceed with extra caution and to make use of all of our skill sets and those of our colleagues and advisors.

These cases also offer abundant opportunity in a practical handbook like this to see how serious some situations can get and how all of the strategies we present in this book come into play.

While attending an event out of state in the middle of October 2019, Joey received an email from a trusted colleague Tonya and he had worked with on several investigations. We often called on one another for advice and to draw on particular areas of research expertise we each have to offer.

A military veteran had contacted our colleague to report all kinds of serious phenomena happening in his home. Not only was his life disrupted to the point that he was sleeping on a recliner in his living room, whatever was manifesting, infesting, and oppressing he and his wife and their home was not content with preying on humans. Two of his cats had died for no reason a veterinarian could discern, a third was now sick, and the man, in his mid-50s and in good health, had recently had a heart attack, which had required three stents and resulted in the death of part of his heart. The doctors were unable to determine the cause of this, as they could find nothing wrong with his heart and all his bloodwork was normal or very close.

It was our colleague's belief that our particular skills and experience made us capable of helping the man and his family. Joey agreed to contact the man to get more information. Several days later, they talked on the phone for thirty minutes, during which Joey confirmed the data already collected by his colleague and gathered further information through a structured interview. It was clear that this family was in danger and in immediate need of help. They had attempted to cope with the phenomena for months—as many people do—but they no longer could. The death of their beloved pets was devastating. The man had further reported that his son, also a veteran, with combat experience in Afghanistan, was having experiences with dark phenomena as well. He had experienced some "nasty stuff" during his time there. He had also told his father that he had had a dream involving a black mist entering his mouth.

Knowing that Tonya's skills as a healer and psychic medium would be invaluable as they were preparing for a site visit, Joey set up a video interview with the man and his wife for the following week. Because of the military background of the man and his son and some consultations the man had had with our colleague and other investigators, the preliminary prognosis was djinn.

Just briefly, *djinn* (from which we get the word "genie") are dark entities prevalent in the Koran and Middle Eastern cultures. They are highly organized, with different colors and traits assigned to a detailed hierarchy. They are shapeshifters and tricksters. According to lore and some firsthand testimony, they can manipulate those in power in business and politics to do their bidding. They are fierce guardians of certain geographical areas. In many ways, they could be termed demons. They also have overlapping traits with faeries and shadow people.

A Not So Subtle Warning to Keep Away

It was clear from the initial phone interview that we were dealing with something dangerous. It would not take long for us to have a personal experience that showed us to what degree. Within half an hour of the phone interview, Joey set up a five-foot, A-frame aluminum ladder to clean the gutters in the front of our house, something he had done dozens of times. As he reached the next to last step at the top, he felt the ladder pulled out from beneath him.

Notice our word choice. It did not fall, or tip over. *It was pulled.* He landed directly on the ladder. Thankfully, he was not seriously hurt. He was winded and in pain, and had narrowly missed being impaled by a broom that was near the ladder, but, other than several large bruises and scrapes on his back and about a week of needing some over-the-counter pain meds and a heating blanket, he fully recovered.

It was clear though that whatever was menacing our new client and his family did not want us getting involved or trying to help.

Despite the forceful warning, we continued our preliminary investigation. The next step was to do further research on the djinn (Joey had been researching them for years and writing about them in his fiction), specifically looking for cases where they attach to those in the military. After revisiting an excellent book on the subject by Rosemary Ellen Guiley, *The Djinn Connection*, we looked at numerous cases available on the Internet. We then consulted with a few military veterans we know who are also paranormal investigators and gleaned additional information through connections other colleagues had.

The Video Interview and a Surprising Revelation

Through Skype, we conducted a one-hour video interview with our client and his wife. Also a military veteran, she was skeptical (and borderline cynical) about all that was reportedly going on, insisting that she had not personally experienced anything. If you remember the continuum we laid out at the start of the book, cynics can be difficult, especially if one or more family members are experiencing phenomena and the people whose support and trust they need are dismissing their experiences. However, in this case, her skepticism was a good thing. It allowed all of us to consider alternate and more mundane explanations and theories from the outset. In other words, to employ our philosophy of CAP—conditional anomalous phenomena. During the video interview, we got more details about some aspects of the case and gathered new data. It is helpful to know, as you saw in the previous case, when the people moved in and when the phenomena began. In this case, they had spent only weekends at the house after initially buying it, but had lived there for about eight years, the first four of which were quiet. They were now thinking about selling the house and building a new one on property they own that is closer to their family business.

We also learned more details about when and how the cats had died, which, in both cases, was due to stomach problems and not eating. One of the cats, which had passed away only two months prior, had gone from twelve to six pounds. We again confirmed that the vet could not provide a medical explanation.

The house was built in the mid-1800s, so we inquired about the possibility of mold. There had been mold, in the attic, when they bought the house, but they had hired specialists to mitigate it. There had also been bat guano, which they removed.

They reported a variety of creaks, snaps, and thuds—the kinds of things you might expect from a 160-year-old house, although they had gotten worse at night as of late and were becoming harder to explain away, even for the wife.

For the past two years, the man had been unable to sleep through the night, waking and getting up every few hours.

By the end of the session, everyone was comfortable enough to agree to a site visit in a few weeks' time.

When Joey ran the GPS for directions to their home a few days later, he was surprised to learn that the house was caddy-corner to a restaurant where we had done a guest investigation and presentation on the art and craft of paranormal field work nine months earlier. The restaurant was extremely active, with evidence of several spirits and ghosts—including a child who liked to play with marbles under the tables in the dining room, a white cat, a cook/cleaning woman, and a dancing girl in tie-dye and dreadlocks playing the bongos who blew some kind of smoke in Joey's face while he was presenting, after which he got a little dizzy and lightheaded! There was also a local gangster named Michael that the restaurant manager often sees in the basement. He reported that something often knocks over boxes and there is sometimes the smell of cigar smoke. This was great confirmation, because Tonya had seen him standing in the basement in suspenders before the presentation and he was smoking a cigar. Michael said his name clearly on the spirit box after first rendering it inoperable for several minutes.

Perhaps he wanted to test us or get to know us a little better before revealing himself in front of the dozens of people in attendance.

Invaluable Guidance from Beyond

With the sobering knowledge that whatever was active in the client's house had already caused harm to several family members and three cats, we spent extra time on our preparation for the site visit. On the morning it was scheduled, Tonya checked in with her spirit guides, whom often provide crucial information. They are aware of things we are not and their high-vibrational energy guides and protects us if we ask.

The session started with her sitting across from a recently deceased mentor who has been invaluable in providing guidance and assisting us with crossing over a variety of ghosts, but Tonya quickly realized that it was not her mentor after all—it was a trickster. It was probably the same entity that had pushed Joey off the ladder, so Tonya's guides quickly got her out of that dangerous psychic space and into a safe zone where the entity could not enter.

They told her that the entity was not a djinn, although they did confirm that djinn attachments are prevalent with Iraq/Afghanistan military veterans.

They also said the entity moved back and forth between the client's house and the restaurant where we had spoken and investigated months before.

Her guides gave her a lot of advice on what to say, what not to say, what to focus on, and offered other suggestions that proved helpful during the site investigation and when clearing the house.

They said that both the son and the man's wife were being oppressed, which corroborated the evidence we had found of oppression during the phone and video interviews—at one point, as they talked about their son, Tonya had even psychically heard the word "oppression."

Her spirit guides confirmed our theory that the entity had targeted the cats because they could sense the entity as it entered and moved around the house. During the site visit we saw the two living cats behaving in a way to confirm that this was indeed true.

The Site Visit

We arrived early on the day of the site visit, parking near the house with a clear view of the restaurant on the opposite corner. Using the EMF meter and a digital tracking device that can detect electromagnetic energy and plot it on a grid, we confirmed that activity was happening between the house and the restaurant. The entity was on the move, perhaps anticipating our visit.

When we entered the house, we sat with the client and his wife in their living room, making a little small talk while we took in the atmosphere. Overall, the energy in the house was pleasant. We asked them for an update since our last conversation. They told us that something had almost knocked the male client out of the recliner he sleeps in at night. It is big and heavy with a broad base and we are confident that he could not have caused what they reported merely by shifting his weight. His wife reported an increase in her pain level in recent weeks (she had some injuries related to her time in the military and she had recently gone from a thirty to eighty percent disability rating). A few nights prior, she had heard her husband arguing with someone in his sleep, with an intensity far beyond his usual nightly mumbling. He had also been having coughing fits and feeling as though something was squeezing his feet.

The man went into more detail about his time in Iraq. He spent part of his tour of duty clearing out underground bunkers. His unit had investigated one in particular because they heard noise coming from it, the source of which they could not identify upon their entry and inspection.

It was when he had come home that his health began to deteriorate.

Although we were told by Tonya's spirit guides that what the family was experiencing was not the work of the djinn, it is important to note that several case histories involving the military and djinn in the Middle East are related to experiences in bunkers. Perhaps the man had encountered djinn, which had opened him up psychically to other types of attacks. The man had brought some objects home with him, including a brass "genie lamp." He was not sure where it was.

Another interesting piece of datum is that, when he had initially spoken to the colleague who referred us, they had talked about djinn, but he could not recall any of the details of that conversation.

Given all of this information, we had been hoping to speak to their son, who had expressed interest in attending, but he was not present during the investigation. More on that later.

During Tonya's session with her spirit guides that morning, they had told her to ask the client and his wife if their son spent a lot of time sleeping on their couch (on which we were now sitting). At first the client said no, although their *grandson* spent a lot of time sleeping there, but then they said that the couch that USED to be there wound up at their son's and he slept on it every night until he wore it out.

Based on our subsequent investigation of the house, which lasted over two hours, it became clear that at least one entity had gone with the couch to the son's house, which may explain the dream of the black mist going into his mouth—he had been sleeping on the couch at the time.

During the investigation, we also identified, through a mix of Tonya's guides' input, the case history, Tonya's psychic mediumship, and the equipment (a spirit box, a digital recorder, a temperature gauge, and an EMF meter) that the entity travels through a mirror that is part of a fireplace mantle that faces an identical mirror on the other side of the room. The husband sleeps every night between them.

No wonder he was having symptoms consistent with night terrors! We are handling an increasing amount of cases where entities are using mirrors as portals. Some of those cases are included in this book.

As we passed the EMF meter slowly over the length of the mirror, it was spiking solid red on one side of it. Neither the other mirror nor any other part of that first mirror showed any EMF activity. Once the investigation was complete, we smudged and covered the mirror and blessed/warded the home. As we did so, the level of energy registering on the EMF meter diminished to mid-range and below until there was finally no EMF reading at all.

But that action was still an hour away. As we went to the second floor to continue the investigation, it was clear that the entity was feeding on the military uniforms and equipment in the room/closet just above where the entrance mirror is. Tonya said touching the uniforms was like watching a war film. One pair of boots, in a duffel bag, had clearly visible bloodstains. We did not ask for details.

Right above that section of the house, in the finished attic, is a storage hatch near the floor. Tonya received a message intuitively that this was where the entity would hide or wait for when the client was asleep in the chair and in a vulnerable state so that it could make its nightly attack.

We advised the client to move the military uniforms and equipment to an area of the house where there was no activity and we put cardboard over the entrance mirror to block the energy flow between that mirror and the one that faced it.

We also advised them to get a mirror to put in the window facing the restaurant to prevent the entity from entering their house.

We also suggested that they purchase sage and palo santo and use them to keep the house smudged (cleared of negative energy). We went over the uses of prayer and spoke a little about how energy flows and the importance of keeping their vibrational energy high.

We had been back on the road for no more than five minutes when we received a call from the client to come back because his son had arrived. He had been picking up his five-year-old son from the boy's mother and he had the boy with him as well.

When we returned to the house, our client said to the boy, "Tell these people what you see at our house."

Boy: A ghost.
Joey: What does it look like?
Boy: Tall and thin and it has sharp teeth and told me it's a vampire. It chases me around.
Joey: Does it have anything on its head?
Boy: A hat.
Joey: (pointing to his grandfather's baseball hat) Like grandpa's?
Boy: No. Like in the circus.

This response made a lot of sense. When we had conducted the video interview, Tonya saw and sketched a tall, thin man in a top hat that she saw standing just behind the client and his wife [see photo].

We did not tell the client about the sketch until after the grandson mentioned the circus hat.

The boy also said the man in the top hat had a long sword. This kind of intimidation, even of children, is typical of a "hat man" or shadow person, a type of dark entity that we had encountered before.

These entities, which investigators do not fully understand (although there are theories that they are related to Middle Eastern djinn, faeries, and alien abductions), prey on fear.

The client's son confirmed his dream of the black mist. It was his belief that it was a demon.

Given the presence of a top-hatted shadow person and the nature of the entity that was traveling in and out of the house through the mirror that categorization is understandable, but there might be an alternative explanation for the black mist.

As we have said, it is important to look for explanations from all possible angles, especially when the family is already in crisis. The black mist might have been a warning from the son's higher self or guides to be careful (he was self-medicating because of his PTSD and his sleep habits were highly disrupted). We shared this with the client, as well as a suggestion to have some energy sessions (Tonya offered to work with him, should he decide to try Reiki), watch his intake of alcohol, and try to get on a healthier sleep schedule. These strategies would help him regardless of what the black mist was, although, because there were no signs of possession and he was not having dark thoughts of violence to himself or others, we were reasonably confident that we were correct.

We are happy to report that the family is doing better. We did not need to return to the house for further clearing and they contacted us about a week after we had left asking for guidance on how to acquire sage and palo santo.

Earned trust and cooperation are essential when it comes to mitigating the ill effects of hauntings.

Generations of Hauntings in a Multi-Family Victorian

Taking the Case History during Our Initial Visit

The case we now report has many overlaps with the previous two, the most prevalent being a family in crisis. Like the previous one, it involves three generations of family, including children.

As we have mentioned, family dynamics and current struggles are a key component to many troublesome hauntings. If you have ever watched Gordon Ramsey's *Kitchen Nightmares*, you will have noticed that the restaurant is usually failing because the family that owns it—and their staff—are in crisis. It is no different with a haunting. Tonya's skills as a trained healer and Joey's as a teacher and mentor are some of the most important in our toolbox in these types of cases. Casual conversation, putting the family at ease, and giving them a break from the chaos are essential.

Having been recommended by a mutual friend while we were visiting their town for the weekend on other business, we had not had the opportunity to speak with anyone in the family prior to our visit, although they felt comfortable enough with our reputation and the word of our mutual friend to agree to do the initial interview in person.

When we arrived at the house, it was obvious that the family was dealing with unusual circumstances. Although the house was your typical sprawling Victorian, every room had more furniture, boxes, and objects than one would expect.

Our first visit was with the owners, a husband and wife. Originally from Honduras, the husband has been in America a long time, having worked for decades in high-level politics in New York City. He has some knowledge of voodoo. The wife is Italian American. She is a sensitive and her family is familiar with the paranormal. Her sister had been the target of black magic from a jealous woman with whose husband she was having an affair and her personality had recently become darker. The man's wife had even cursed members of the family and our new client said her family was feeling the effects of the curse.

Their five-year-old granddaughter was with us for a few minutes, but they obviously could not talk openly in front of her and we were careful what we said as well. Their daughter, who was going through a divorce, had moved in a few months prior with her three children (there were also two boys, teen and pre-teen, who were out that day; the daughter was at work) and brought all of her furniture and belongings with her. That explained why the house was so crammed. The matriarch kept apologizing. It was not how she normally kept her home and we could see that she was under stress.

The start of our investigation centered on the fireplace in the living room where we were gathered. It was not original to the home. The homeowners had rescued it from a house that had caught fire. It was clear that there was a woman, whom Tonya identified as "Emily," who was attached to the fireplace.

There were also other old objects, such as a chandelier from the 1920s, which they had added to their home.

The history of a home can tell you a lot about what is going on. In this case, there was plenty—the owners were well informed and it was a great help in sorting things out, because there were not only multiple families living in the house—there were many spirits and ghosts, some of whom were related.

As far as the family's connection to it, the house was abandoned for seventeen years before the family bought it. Almost as soon as they moved in, they began to hear noises and experience other phenomena. The wife had seen a man whom she knew was attached to the house. She was sure he was not happy that they had bought it and moved in.

Soon after she reported this, Tonya saw a man in a top hat in the next room—once a dining room, it was now a storage area—peeking out from behind a piece of antique furniture. He was unhappy that Tonya could see him. He had built the house and had been a schoolteacher.

As Tonya reported this, the wife confirmed that she had also seen him. He hid in the attic. Naturally generous, the family matriarch had invited someone else to stay with them at an earlier point in time, and the guest's bed was in the attic. The man had laughed maniacally in her ear one night. On another night, he had told her to wake up the family patriarch because the chimney was on fire.

It was.

Intrigued by this man, who exhibited a wide range of personality traits, we encouraged them to tell us more. He had not only built the house—he had also helped to build a church down the street (which is still there). He was a respected community leader. Then it all went bad. During a dispute with the church elders, they accused him of homosexual activity and the congregation, forced to choose, abandoned him. (Tonya confirmed with him that this was indeed the case.) Having lost almost everything, he had hung himself in his barn (which is no longer there).

As if this was not enough tragedy for one man to bear, the story continued. He had loved his apple orchard. His daughter had gotten married on their property. After he died, there was an accident—the daughter's husband was cutting a tree, which fell on him. He died in one of the front rooms of the house.

The daughter's tragedies continued. Her father's brother tried to take the property away from her after her husband's death by suing her. She walked *seventeen miles* to the courthouse to make a plea to keep the property.

She won.

As you can see, the original owners had a deep connection to the property, to a large degree forged and sealed with their blood, though the tragedies continued for many years to come. Two children had died in the house: an eight-year-old who died of pneumonia and a baby less than eighteen months old.

Emily and the owner were not the only ones haunting the house. The wife had seen a burly worker in jeans, a work hat, and a blade of grass in his mouth. And not in her mind's eye. He was a full-bodied, solid apparition. The family also reported, and Tonya confirmed, a female ghost with a high-waisted black skirt, peach shirt with puffy sleeves, and a high neck.

In addition to the ghosts and spirits, there were plenty of other haunting phenomena. Water faucets turned on by themselves in the bathroom and the kitchen. People in other areas of the house would hear the piano play, but no one (living) was near it. The family reported other noises for which they could not account.

They had also seen a swirling white light so bright the granddaughter, asleep on the couch, had rubbed her eyes. They had heard a sound like radio static as the white light disappeared into a heating grate. On another occasion, they saw a sparkling shape twinkling and moving in the living room.

At this point in the interview, perhaps because they were now feeling comfortable with us, they reported that a ghost had thrown a toy airplane at the grown daughter's neck. She was also pushed down the stairs. The eighteen-year-old girl who had been staying in the attic of the house, whom the original owner did not like, was also shoved on the stairs.

The most concerning phenomenon to us, because it was still happening, was that neither of the boys could sleep—one had been in a sleep study program and the doctors found no cause for his waking up so often during the night. Not knowing what else to do, they had recently prescribed him tranquilizers.

Forty-five minutes into the interview, as we prepared to shift gears and do a room-by-room investigation, it was clear that the deaths, struggles, and attachments had made the property a powerful generator for manifestations and paranormal phenomena.

Having already spent a little time in or near the rooms on the first floor—the kitchen, living room, and dining room—we decided to focus our efforts on the upstairs, where a good bit of the most alarming experiences had taken place. Tonya was sure that this was where the man in the top hat was hiding.

We had no sooner started to climb the stairs where the two girls had been pushed than the EMF meter began to show moderate activity and the spirit box flashed red, both indicating the presence of a ghost or spirit.

Expecting to find the man in the top hat, as we reached the top of the stairs what greeted us instead was the ghost of a woman in her seventies or eighties with wild grey hair, who was cranky and mean. She was behaving erratically, and Tonya felt strongly that she had dementia. It was also clear that she was the one keeping the boys up at night, poking them and moving the covers. The bedroom where the older one was staying might have been hers and she was confused about why he was in her space.

Does this sound familiar? It is not that different from the young man who committed suicide wondering who the people in his parents' house were.

The longer we spent upstairs, the more agitated the ghost of the old woman became. We had also been with the family for well over an hour and the daughter and her two sons were due to arrive near dinner time, so we decided to end our investigation and set up a time to return in the near future to help cross the old woman over and otherwise settle the activity in the house.

Before we left, as a way to help create some calm before we returned, we did a ceremony outside the house with ceremonial tobacco and sage—warding the property at its boundaries, asking for protection for the family, and putting white light around them.

Due to return in less than a week, we took the opportunity to do further research online and to seek help from a historian from their part of the state with whom we had worked in the past. Together we confirmed many of the details of the family that had originally owned the home through online sites like Find a Grave and digitized county records.

We also prepared to attempt to cross over the old woman with dementia.

Our Return Visit

As is sometimes the case, activity had increased instead of decreased inside the home after our initial visit. The man in the top hat was agitated that Tonya had seen him. Perhaps others were agitated as well, such as the woman with dementia. A door in the kitchen had been opening and closing on its own. Baskets and plates that had been hanging on the kitchen wall for years had fallen one night around 2 am and some were broken. The husband and wife heard footsteps just prior to that happening. There was knocking on the bathroom door upstairs, but no one was there. Their daughter had seen a human-shaped shadow pass the shower curtain one evening as she was showering in there.

The good news was that no one had been pushed or had anything thrown at them or had otherwise been in danger.

Committed to our plan to cross the woman with dementia over, we chose the bedroom where she tormented the boys as our base. We burned sage, ceremonial tobacco, and rosemary in a bowl and asked for assistance in crossing the woman over. A longtime mentor who had recently died joined us and indicated that we needed to go into the bathroom. Keeping the herbs burning, we received instructions from our mentor to play 1940s music to lure the woman into the space. Within seconds, the ghost entered and began to sing along. Our mentor appeared in the bathroom mirror and enticed the ghost to join her, where there was a vibrant party happening attended by people the ghost had known.

We soon received confirmation from our mentor that the woman had crossed over and our work for the evening was done. As a second confirmation, we asked her to light the temperature light on the spirit box, which she did.

While the resident ghosts and spirits in the house may be there for years to come—their attachments are certainly both legitimate and strong—things have settled down considerably for this family, and we were happy to learn upon following up with them that the boys were sleeping better. Three generations all living in the same crowded space, adjusting to a life-changing experience like a divorce and each making sacrifices and having to compromise on some level each and every day, is enough to deal with without being harassed and interfered with by those no longer living.

Bringing them some peace, while also helping the woman with dementia find her way to where she belonged, made for a happy ending in this particular case.

All in the Family

As you can see by the cases we've thus far shared, there is quite a bit involved in a paranormal investigation of a haunted home. There is interplay between the living and the dead, the history of the house and land is usually a factor, and there is rarely one phenomenon; most importantly, there is often more than one ghost, spirit, or entity, and they all have different needs, motivations, and intentions.

It gets even more complicated when you are related to or are friends with the people involved. In these situations, it is much harder to prevent your knowledge of the people and the place from distorting your interpretation. In Remote Viewing circles, analysts call this "analytic overlay," or AOL (an acronym created by Ingo Swann, the acknowledged father of Remote Viewing). AOL occurs when our conscious mind distorts the facts by overlaying the information we already know onto those facts and the circumstances of the situation. This is one reason that Tonya prefers to know as little as possible about a client and property before beginning an investigation.

So, when a close friend we had known for many years and his new girlfriend brought us into their newly acquired home when they felt an uptick in activity, we knew the case would have these challenges. However, given that there were no signs of *infestation* or *oppression*—in other words, whatever was happening was not threatening them—we thought it would be an interesting case to accept.

The background of the case was also relatively simple. While visiting his family, our friend was gifted by a relative a chair that had been in the family going back to the time of the US Civil War. It was not long after his return that he put the chair in his basement office and went about his business. Soon after, though, he and his girlfriend noticed that their cat acted oddly near the chair and then they found an answer—they both sensed a woman sitting in it. That is when they invited us to spend the weekend with them to see what we could find.

Through psychic mediumship, use of a spirit box, asking many questions of our friend, and real-time online research on genealogy and Civil War websites, we discovered that the woman in the chair was our friend's ancestor. During our investigation, she kept pointing at the girlfriend, and Tonya was hearing a letter of the alphabet. We thought the ghost was trying to indicate her own name, and she was, but spirits and ghosts with their full faculties tend to be much more efficient than the living. Not only was she indicating the first letter of her own name, she was using the shortened version of the name of the girlfriend (and for a specific reason we did not figure out until later)! Not knowing the girlfriend well, it took a while to figure out. Turns out the shortened version was the nickname her mother used when the girlfriend was little.

The ghost (let's call her Carolin) was also showing Tonya her dress, smoothing out the skirt over and over. Perhaps it was to help us figure out the right era in which she lived. Carolin was also indicating that she was waiting for something. She showed Tonya a number of objects: a letter, a trunk, a family bible with a brown leather cover and gold letters, and a fan. Our friend confirmed that the fan was still in the family. As we worked with Carolin, she was able to provide answers to Yes/No questions with the EMF meter. There was a warm spot in the center of the chair—66 degrees elsewhere, up to 80 degrees on the chair.

It took several hours, but we were also able to figure out what Carolin was waiting for. Her daughter, *whose name was similar to the girlfriend's childhood nickname*, had died of scarlet fever when she was nineteen. Carolin felt as though no one had properly acknowledged her daughter's death. We did our best to remedy that oversight immediately by expressing our condolences.

Since that night, Carolin has truly become part of their family. They moved her chair from the basement to the upstairs living area. They leave books for her to read (turning the pages each morning) and her chair is in a place of honor. They also have a desk from another relative that even contains some of the tools he used for his trade and the area around it is active as well.

Using the Xbox Kinect, a tool used by an increasing amount of researchers, they were able to record a stick figure image of Carolin in the chair. While some skeptics say that the Kinect looks for patterns in the weave of the fabric or the natural shape of a chair, when we reviewed the video recording, we could clearly see the arm made by the Kinect figure move and place its "hand" over the girlfriend's as she placed it on the arm of the chair.

We could use more of these happy endings when it comes to haunted homes.

Although, in our friend's case, this is not the end of the story.

As sometimes happens after investigators have opened wider a virtual door in the psychic space through attention to a haunting—especially using energy-measuring instruments and a psychic medium—the activity in their home expanded to different phenomena.

One night, about a month later, we were sitting outside enjoying some conversation and a takeout meal on their back deck when our friend suddenly got an odd look on his face, stood up without comment, and staggered toward the screen door. His girlfriend managed to open the door and guide him inside before he collapsed, close to passing out.

We at first thought it might have been the food, but we all ordered the same meal and everyone else was fine. Our friend described a strange energy that had suddenly overtaken him. Tonya did some Reiki to clear his energetic field and within fifteen minutes he was fine, if not shaken. We all were. Considering that we had been spending most of the day and evening watching shows about the paranormal and talking about various cases, we were pretty sure that something not nice had "caught the scent" and seized an opportunity.

A few months later, they called to say that there was odd activity happening in their basement and on the stairs leading to it. Their cat had started going to the bathroom upstairs instead of going down to the litter box—recall a similar situation in the case of the young man who had committed suicide—and, although our friend's office was in the basement, he had never felt comfortable down there and had never decorated or otherwise made it his own. There were still moving boxes around the room even though they had been living there for over a year. He found himself spending less and less time in the basement and he had seen, on a few occasions, a dark shadow near the stairs. Carolin, whose chair they had moved from her accustomed spot in the dining room to about four feet away from the basement stairs during the Christmas holiday season when they had put up their tree, was becoming agitated at times as well.

Soon after we arrived, we brought our equipment into the basement and immediately began to receive communications through the spirit box and a digital communication app on a smartphone. We heard or saw the words, "office," "bound," and "Germany." We asked several questions and were able to eliminate the possibility that it was our friend's ancestor whose objects were in the desk. Tonya then saw a ghost of a man who identified as "Johnny." He said, "It's quiet" (the basement certainly was) and "unbothered." It took a little time, as he seemed to be very much at home and not interested in leaving but, with the help of Archangel Michael, Tonya was able to cross Johnny over. This brings up an interesting point. Just because a ghost or spirit is not harming or threatening you does not mean you necessarily want them in your space. And please note that we did not try to *banish* Johnny. Tonya tried and succeeded in *crossing him over*. As she did, the digital communication app flashed the word "Thanks." What a great confirmation.

Because, as sometimes happens, he could have refused to go.

Which was what we encountered next.

After Johnny had gone, Tonya sensed another man. This one was not at all friendly and did not care to communicate. After some group cooperation and concentration, we realized that there was a black scrying mirror on a shelf in the basement. Although our friend kept it covered with a cloth, transient spirits were still utilizing it to come in and out. Johnny had been one and this nameless man was another. Having been taught how to use a scrying mirror by someone who had not only used them extensively but had learned to make them and train others in their use, we did a ritual to keep the mirror closed when it was not in use by the owner.

Tonya was again able to call on Archangel Michael to get the nameless man out of the space.

We are happy to report that the cat has been using the basement litter box ever since and our friend has "claimed" the space by decorating it and spending more time there.

You have to wonder if this is why basements and attics tend to be haunted. It could be a combination of the fact that they typically have lots of random objects, some of which might be haunted and they also in many cases act as storage and not living spaces, which may invite "squatters" or those, like Johnny, who want a place where "it's quiet" and they are "unbothered."

Joey has noticed that the activity in our current home's basement subsided once he put a desk and several bookshelves down there for a writing room.

If you are having trouble with activity in a basement or attic, try claiming the space as your own. Personalizing a space imprints our unique energy signature onto it, perhaps making it less energetically "available."

A Basement and Bedroom Intruder

A few years ago, a client of Tonya's relayed some encounters he experienced as a child growing up in Chicago. He came to Tonya hoping to gain some insight into troubling experiences he had had in his childhood home. These experiences continued into his adult life and he had been seeking answers to what was behind these experiences his entire life.

Michael (a pseudonym) explained that he had grown up in a house that always aroused in him a sense of "evil" and foreboding. As a child, he always felt as if someone or something was watching him intently and consequently he never felt at ease in the house. It never felt to him like a home. The sense of foreboding and the sensation of being watched were so strong that Michael took every opportunity to be outside, frequently staying overnight with friends.

Michael had a difficult time sleeping in his room, particularly because it was at night that the sense of foreboding and sensation of something watching him were the strongest. He shared that, as a child, he had spent many nights lying awake in his bed, covers pulled over his face, with just his eyes peeking out from beneath the blankets. One evening in particular he was feeling exceptionally on edge, and as he lay in his bed watching the moonlight stream in through his bedroom curtains, he began to see the outline of a figure, whom he said at first reminded him of Christ.

Michael recalled that he could see the faint outline of what appeared to be a crown of thorns and thought that the figure had its arms extended toward him. This confused Michael and he remembered thinking, "Jesus doesn't come in the dark. Jesus only comes in the light." At that moment, the thorny crown morphed into what appeared to be two horns. As this happened, Michael heard a voice in his mind telling him to go under the covers and count to three.

Years later, while reflecting on the incident, Michael surmised that three represented the Holy Trinity, and that the information had come to him from a guide or angel. Michael did as the voice instructed and when he peered out from beneath the covers, the figure was gone.

Malevolent and demonic entities will sometimes mimic children or someone you love in order to gain your trust. It is always important to rely on your gut instinct when encountering apparitions and it was fortunate for Michael that he trusted his instincts that evening.

Years later, as an adult, Michael had another encounter while he was home visiting his parents. One evening, Michael had gone out drinking with some childhood friends. When he returned later that night, he was quite inebriated and decided to sleep in the basement so he did not disturb his parents by going to his upstairs bedroom. As Michael made himself comfortable on a cot, which was set up on the far side of the basement, his sense of unease was so overwhelming that he decided to keep the light on. Michael recalled that each time he would begin to dose off, the light switching off would awaken him, and each time he turned the light back on it would switch back off within a matter of moments. It was at that point that Michael said he felt a dark and malicious presence in the basement with him. He sensed a figure standing just behind the line of freshly washed laundry hanging on a line just next to his cot. Michael had had enough. He made a quick retreat upstairs to his bedroom.

When Tonya shared with Michael that her guides were showing her that some type of ritualistic occultism had occurred in the attic of the home prior to his family moving in, he shared the following: "After I moved away, I rarely came to visit because I felt so uneasy in the home. One of the few times I did return, I felt compelled to go up into the attic. In the corner, I found what appeared to be a baby's skull. I thought I must be mistaken and I left it where it was. I couldn't stop thinking about it though, so before I asked my mother if she knew anything about it, I wanted to go back up to look at it again to be sure. When I went back up to the attic, it was gone."

It was at this point that Tonya shared with Michael that she was not just being shown the dark presence in his home, but that a doorway had been opened that served as a portal, allowing all manner of beings to enter the house. She was being shown that the portal affected the houses on either side of Michael's, extending as far as three or four houses on either side.

Michael felt this made sense and shared that as a child he had been on a few occasions in the neighbor's basement and sensed the same evil and foreboding that he sensed in his parents' house.

To this day, Michael's mother (his father has since passed), resides in that home and Michael, as much as he regrets not seeing his mother, is reluctant to go there to visit.

Michael's story could very well be a segment on one of the paranormal reality shows like *My Paranormal Nightmare*. It has all the classic elements, or tropes—a child who is able to see entities, especially at night in their bedroom, and an escalation of the activity as time progresses. There are even the elements of the basement and the attic—places that are less trafficked than other rooms in the house—places of transience filled with boxes and not "personalized" with decorations, paintings and photos, and knick-knacks.

Michael's story also illuminates the dangers of dark magic activities such as satanic rituals and opening portals. Once these doorways are open, they are difficult to close and it is all but impossible to regulate what comes through them. Without closing the portal, attempts to clear the house will prove to be temporary, just like if you have a hole in the screen door and flies are getting in. You might be able to kill the ones in the house, but there are plenty more still getting in.

Helping a Friend with a Follow-Home

People frequently ask us if it is possible for ghosts or other entities to attach themselves to you, and/or follow you home. Not only is this possible, it is a fairly common occurrence. We talked about some of our own experiences with follow-homes earlier in the book. This is why we strongly suggest cleansing your energy field before re-entering your home after you have been out, particularly if you have been in or near locations known for being active, or for having heavy or unsettling energy. Locations that paranormal investigators return to with regularity are typically the places one thinks of first, with the obvious graveyards, caves, prisons, and abandoned asylums coming to mind.

Rarely does one imagine such a location to be their place of employment.

Several years ago, a close friend asked Tonya to see if she could sense anything unusual in her home. Her friend (whom we will call Beth) had always enjoyed clear, bright energy in her house, but she had suddenly noticed a heavy and foreboding energy in her once peaceful place of residence. Beth was having trouble sleeping and would often wake in the middle of the night with a strong sense of something watching her. Tonya had stayed with Beth on quite a few occasions, so she was surprised to hear of the change in energy and wondered if something had followed her friend home. If so, Tonya suspected Beth's place of work as the potential source, because of the history of the building, which was formerly a hospital. Tonya had also spent enough time in that building to know that it had a very heavy and foreboding energy.

Beth was out of town when Tonya had the opportunity to visit her home to see what she could pick up about what might be going on. She arrived around nine in the evening and instantly sensed what her friend had been describing. Tonya had been alone at Beth's home many times before and had never experienced the apprehensive and uneasy feelings that arose when she arrived on that particular evening. Immediately after entering the foyer, Tonya felt as if something was watching her. In fact, the feeling was so strong that Tonya's hackles instantly went up and her initial impulse was to turn on her heels and leave. As she entered the house, she heard strange rustling noises coming from the kitchen. Combined with her feeling of danger upon entering, the noise from the kitchen had Tonya wondering if she was hearing an intruder.

Dismissing this idea, she entered the kitchen to investigate but could find nothing to explain the source of the sounds. As she left the kitchen, the sensation of someone standing directly behind her was so strong that she considered calling another friend who lived close by to see if she might consider coming over. Not wanting to worry the neighbor, Tonya dismissed the idea for the moment, and instead decided to sit on the back deck long enough to regain her bearings and muster up some courage.

The evening was warm and clear and Tonya sat gazing at the star-filled sky. The atmosphere outside was remarkably different—there was a gentle breeze and everything felt calm and peaceful, the way the inside of her friend's house had always felt in the past. After about ten minutes, Tonya felt confident enough to re-enter the house. The moment she did, however, she felt her body go back into full alert as the intense sensation of something watching her rushed over her again. In that moment, she decided that she was not safe alone in the house and dialed her nearby friend, who did not answer. It was now nearly 10 pm, and Tonya assumed that her friend had gone to bed, so she resolved to go upstairs and do the same. Before she did, she called Beth to find out where she kept her sage bundle, so that she could cleanse and ward the house before retiring.

As they talked, she shared with Beth the overwhelming feelings of something watching her and described the sounds from the kitchen. Beth indicated that these were the exact experiences that she had been having and directed Tonya to the sage in her master bathroom. As Tonya walked through the master bedroom on her way to retrieve the sage, she not only noticed the strong sensation of being watched intensify—she was finally able to discover its source. There, standing near the foot of the bed, was the ghost of a tall, gangly man in a tattered brown suit. Tonya was immediately able to see his connection to Beth's place of employment, the former hospital building. It was clear he had followed her friend home from work. Although his energy was not evil or malevolent, it had a strange, foreboding quality that Tonya sensed had something to do with the manner in which he had died. Evidently, he had found something interesting about Beth. Tonya retrieved the sage from the bathroom closet and went to work smudging the house and instructing the man to leave. She informed him that he could either return to the old hospital building, or cross over, but that he was not welcome in the house. Tonya also called on Archangel Michael for assistance in removing the man from the home, and after smudging every room in the house while repeating a prayer to St. Michael, she felt the energy in the house returning to normal. The sense of uneasiness was gone and Tonya was able to breathe a sigh of relief, go to sleep, and enjoy a peaceful night's rest.

Tonya followed up with Beth frequently afterward to make sure that the man did not follow her home again. She also suggested that Beth take precautions upon returning home from work each day. In order to cleanse her energy field, and clear any potential attachments from her work environment, Tonya recommended that Beth surround herself in protective white light each morning before work, and to reinforce the protective bubble around her in the middle of her workday. Tonya also suggested wearing or bringing stones such as tiger's eye and black obsidian to work, as these stones serve to dispel negative energies. Last, Tonya recommended that her friend shower or bathe with Epsom salts immediately upon her return from work, as salt water cleanses and neutralizes negative energies. To this day, the house remains calm and peaceful, and her friend has had no further encounters.

We always recommend taking the protective measures that Tonya shared with her friend before visiting any active location, or beginning an investigation. Calling on your guides and angels to assist and protect you while you are at such locations is also an important habit to develop.

Buyer Beware

Another of Tonya's friends contacted her to request a distance reading for her home. Ramona (a pseudonym) had recently purchased a house that she and her husband were looking forward to renovating. Despite her original excitement about the house, once she and her family had moved in, Ramona found that she felt extremely uncomfortable there. There was a dark and heavy energy about it despite the beautiful aesthetic. The all-too-common sensation of something watching them was accompanied by mild disturbances, which eventually escalated into light bulbs shattering with no visible or scientific explanation.

Upon connecting with Ramona and viewing the home remotely, Tonya noticed a solemn man in a black suit. While the man did not necessarily seem malevolent, he was unhappy and unfriendly. It was Tonya's sense that he felt connected to the home and was not at all happy about sharing it with Ramona and her family. Tonya tried to communicate with him to ask him to leave. However, he was not interested in communication.

Tonya suggested smudging the home with sage and palo santo and worked remotely over several months clearing the home with Reiki symbols and energies. Over time, the energy in the house improved and the family could no longer detect the spirit of the man. The house does continue to have some issues that Tonya attributes to *Feng Shui*, which is an ancient Chinese practice that works to maintain an energy balance between living spaces and the natural environment. The orientation of Ramona's house and the land on which it is built contribute to continued areas of unbalance, both in the house and in Ramona's life.

Although Tonya was able to offer some Feng Shui remedies for the house, the placement of the structure on the property and the way it affects the energies that flow to and from the house is a challenge that is hard to overcome. Tonya recommended to Ramona that she sell the house in order to restore balance to her life. This was something Tonya did not take lightly. Selling a house and uprooting a family are drastic measures and something we only recommend when it is clear that the challenges faced by the family cannot be overcome with the other strategies and practices described in this book.

Ramona's case is another example of not trusting your gut instinct. Although the house itself was beautiful, in a great location and priced right, it never felt "right" to Ramona, who has a great deal of natural intuitive ability. Because she could not quite place her finger on the source of her uneasiness, she chose to ignore it. As a result, the house never felt like a home.

We strongly recommend doing some research on Feng Shui before buying or renting a house. Check the direction of the house and placement of the rooms against a Feng Shui Bagua Map, and, as always, be sure to trust any gut feelings you have upon your first inspection of the house.

We certainly learned this the hard way with the Tinton Falls, New Jersey house. The first time we went to look at it, although newly remodeled and charming, we could not shake the uneasy feeling we felt while walking through its rooms.

If possible, it is also important to learn something about the history of the house. Many hauntings and disturbances occur, not because of the location or the actual house itself, but because of activities engaged in or experiences had by previous occupants, such as with Michael's family home or the multifamily Victorian. It is always helpful to learn anything you can about the residents who preceded you. A quick trip to the local library, town hall, or historical society can yield a lot of information. With the Leavittsburg house, knowing the name of the man who built it after researching the deed and other property records helped us with our communication. Just being able to say his name was a big help in creating a relationship.

Asking neighbors is always a good way to gather information, as is searching archived newspapers for stories about your home address.

Part III: More from Our Case Files: Haunted Buildings/Places of Business

Our Old Friend, the Webb, Morehead City, North Carolina

There is no question that the Webb Memorial Library and Convention Center had a profound, lasting impact on many of the more than five hundred people who joined us as either part of our investigation team, as one-time guests, or those who returned several times during the time we spent there.

During the two years of the investigation, visitors experienced a wide variety of spiritual and paranormal phenomena. Some were contacted by their deceased loved ones. Others, who did not know they had psychic ability, were suddenly seeing ghosts, spirits, and other entities. At least three men who came in as skeptics left believing that there was more to all of this than they thought when they heard voices in their ear or their name spoken on the spirit box. Some were so frightened they had to leave, getting considerably more than they bargained for when they signed up. Others reported having something follow them home, creating a disturbance in their residence for a day or two—or longer, such as was the case with the woman who took home a silver dollar that had appeared out of nowhere one night that terrorized her dog for several weeks, until her husband brought the coin to the bank. Some visitors burst into tears while they were there, while others received messages of advice, hope, and warning from Dr. Thompson.

Our book on the two-year investigation is comprehensive in its coverage of what others and we experienced there and we do not wish to repeat ourselves. We have chosen to include the Webb in the current book because of the strange array of experiences that former guests—and readers with psychic ability who had never been there—experienced after *Watch Out for the Hallway* was published in September 2018.

We talked about the uptick in paranormal activity in our own home and lives after the book was published, but we quickly learned that we were not alone.

One guest who participated in the Webb investigation several times and who has since become a friend and colleague wrote to us within a month of the book coming out. We had sent her a complimentary, autographed copy as a thank you for some of her contributions to it.

She wound up having several odd experiences after the book arrived. First, shortly after she read the story about the silver dollar we mentioned above, she was standing at the teller window at the bank when a quarter rolled right beside her and stopped. She glanced around. No one was looking and no one had dropped the coin. She looked at it and heard, "Do not pick it up."

This was just the start. A few nights later, when she went to bed, she could hear talking, as though it was coming from deep within a tunnel. Another night, at 2:44 am (an active hour for paranormal phenomena), she was awakened by something standing over and beside her. The left side of her head felt like she was being electrocuted. This was most likely because of a spike in electromagnetic energy as the entity was manifesting.

As the days passed, the activity picked up. Even her husband, who was not reading the book, was noticing. While he was in the shower one morning, he heard a voice tell him not to use the hot water. There was a night he woke up feeling as though something was standing over him or staring at him from down the hallway. She was skeptical because there is a large bookshelf at the end of the hallway that can play tricks on the eye and mind when it's dark. But then, the following day, he was home alone and had to go sit out on the front porch because the activity was so bad. He told her he saw a figure move from under the doorway to the bathroom that had frightened him. That night, she fell asleep in the couch because neither of them had been sleeping well. She woke up and there was a figure standing over her, close enough for her to feel it invading her space. She chose to ignore it and go back to sleep. Not long after, her husband woke up panicked and asked her to sleep in the bed with him because something was in the bedroom. At about 2:45 am that morning (note again the time) their bedroom television turned on with the volume turned up high. It got worse. What they saw was an adult movie on a premium cable channel. The remote was nowhere near them. Neither one of them had been watching that channel, nor would they have the television at that volume. They unplugged it from the wall and slept for a few more hours before she was awakened by the sensation of something grabbing her backside, causing her to scream.

Because she was by now a veteran of the paranormal, she was not afraid; she knew whatever it was wanted their attention and not to harm them. It certainly did have boundary issues, as did a few of the ghosts from the Webb.

Another unfortunate aspect of the haunting was that her deceased grandparents, who often visited her, were not coming around anymore. This is a phenomenon that we also witnessed at the Webb and elsewhere. Like the living, the deceased often will not share space with another deceased ghost or spirit that is aggravating them. Her husband had gotten used to the activity of the grandparents but this was something new and therefore upsetting.

The new phenomena also included her feeling a cold spot on her arm while in bed. She eliminated the ceiling fan as the culprit after a series of tests. Her pets, which would not get upset when the grandparents were around, were avoiding the bedroom.

This is interesting. Not only can pets detect spirits, ghosts, and other entities—they can discern between benevolent and malevolent ones.

Our friend lent her copy of the book to another person who had come with us to the Webb multiple times. After she did so, the atmosphere in her home changed for the better. Her grandparents even returned once she had loaned the book and she reported that there were now other presences, of a "light energy," there as well.

To this day, the book remains with her friend, who keeps it in the garage.

Soon after the book came out, she also purchased a copy for a friend who is a sensitive. Although she had forgotten, her friend reminded her that she had had a dream prior to the book's publication where they were in the library together. Her friend had never been there. They were holding hands as our friend guided her through the library. They entered a room with a chair in it that was upholstered with a high-quality leather substitute. The room also had a table. She said the other furniture in the room looked old but had been redone (this was most likely what we called the Meeting Room). In the corner was a man with a burned face. She tried to talk to him and said that he was stubborn and did not want to leave (this event happened almost exactly like this to us a few times at the Webb—it had been a triage at times during World War II when German U-boats attacked oil tankers on the North Carolina coast). Our friend led her out of the room and down a hallway and she heard "We cannot go down there" and the dream ended as her friend started to say, "Just…"

Her friend reported to her that, as she was flipping through the book when she first received it, she came to the picture of what we called the "North Hallway." That was the hallway from her dream. Readers of *Watch Out for the Hallway* know that the North Hallway gives the book its title. One night while we were dealing with a group of angry male ghosts and other phenomena like spectral Men in Black and an interdimensional being in that area we were warned by Dr. Thompson to "Watch out for the hallway."

Having not read the book or ever been on the investigations, her friend had no way of knowing what turned out to be very accurate information given to her in a dream.

The sensitive was so frightened she closed the book and left it unread for a while. She did eventually read the book and had some other psychic experiences with other rooms and events.

Although things calmed down in her house, our frequent guest reported that, for about a week, she had been having a strong urge to drive to the library, even hearing voices telling her to. Friday was the strongest day. This was interesting because that was always our most popular night as far as number of guest investigators and things would always be very active. Not able to resist the urge that day, she started the drive and began to feel weak and dizzy. The voices and urge continued but as she felt worse, she overcame them. In the days that followed, she had dizzy spells, nausea, and even fell down once.

She also reported lack of appetite followed by ravenous hunger and a persistent fatigue.

As we report in *Hallway*, we both had dreams where someone or something pulled us to the library. There is no question that there were ghosts and spirits that resided there that liked the attention they received those two years and missed it.

It also reminds us of a situation a colleague at a witchcraft museum shared with us. Part of their collection is a supposed dybbuk box (popularized on the Internet a few years ago, these are holding vessels sealed with wax and warded with sigils that supposedly contain an evil spirit of some kind; the dybbuk is a demon from the Jewish tradition). There is no question that the energy around the box is sour and strong. Joey felt nauseous any time he got within six feet of it. One day, a man went into the museum saying he was driving past and heard a voice tell him to go into the museum and buy the box. Keep in mind, the man had never been there before and did not know the box existed until the voice spoke to him. The man offered cash and when the curator refused, he pulled out his credit card and doubled the number. The curator still refused, although it was a considerable amount of money that the fledgling museum could surely use. As demonstrated time and again in this book, dark entities are persistent opportunists. They are always on the prowl for someone in a vulnerable moment that they can try to get to do their bidding.

During the first few months after *Hallway* came out, we heard from others that had spent more than one evening with us at the Webb. One wrote in an email, "I started to read the book the night before last and I felt like someone was watching me the whole time. So much so that I got goosebumps."

Another texted, "Things have become louder than words [his way of saying that the phenomena was strong] since I have read the book. What the heck? Someone/thing is PISSED. I almost feel as if Pandora opened her box."

And then there was an email from a woman who thought that one of the ghosts that had been consistently communicating with us for the first year of the investigation and then crossed over had followed her home. She said that he was not being difficult or insulting, as he had been to women when we first met him, but that he was being a caregiver and even protective one Halloween night. This was consistent with the change in his personality as Tonya and others worked with him over the course of our visits. When this person had joined us, the first of two times, she had heard on the P-SB11 the word "personal" and felt it was about her. She had found out prior to her visit that one of the two doctors that had offices downstairs in the 1920s was her childhood friend's great grandfather.

A Very Haunted Historical Society Museum

Imagine an attic crammed full with objects from several centuries, including: artifacts from doctors' offices; uniforms, knapsacks, and weapons from the military; puppets (which move almost daily although they are behind glass), marionettes, and dolls; articles of clothing (there is an older woman attached to a display of hats); and a wide variety of other types of artifacts and antiques. As we have demonstrated several times in this book, all of the above are items that are well known to propagate hauntings.

Now imagine that attic being 36,000 square feet and spread over three stories.

In May 2019, and again several months later, we had the opportunity to do an investigation of just such a place. We encountered numerous ghosts and spirits. One was a Mennonite who stayed by the property's apple orchard. There was also a blond-headed three- year-old boy and a quiet man attached to a piano (the curator and board members had heard it play at times). Perhaps the most unique of them all was a man in military uniform with a wicked sense of humor who lured Tonya into the basement, where there was a creepy doll around a corner in a disturbing pose just waiting to make her jump with fright. This was something he had done before—no wonder the curator and another investigator were sharing a quiet laugh between them as Tonya followed the ghost.

There was also a residual haunting that was powerful enough to cross a pair of dowsing rods.

In addition to the three-year-old, there was another boy, about eight years old, whose name is Tommy, on a different floor. Tommy liked to play on and around a pair of barbershop chairs. His electromagnetic signature also spiked around a display case of Boy Scout badges. He was excited to show us the two-story-tall clock tower mechanism, which is all shiny brass and gears. A little boy's dream!

Although the curator and staff kept the museum meticulously maintained, there were places in the building that had a dark, dangerous energy. In most other areas the energy was more neutral but strong, sometimes to the point of activating Joey's solar plexus.

As you have read in some of our other cases, both in this book and in *Watch Out for the Hallway*, phenomena often appear in bathrooms, and at least one of the museum's bathrooms was no exception. There had been reports of women smelling curry when they used the ladies room. Sure enough, Tonya saw an Indian woman wearing a sari and bindi during our first visit. She also smelled curry. She was unable to glean any information about why the ghost was in the bathroom or what she needed. All Tonya knew was that the woman did not want to be there. She was trapped.

One of the areas that felt dark and dangerous was near to where the young boy upstairs, Tommy, liked to play. We soon learned why. There was a former superintendent of the building (it had formerly been what is called a "poor farm") who haunted its hallways, believing he was still in charge. Tonya describes him as being tall and gaunt, with sunken eyes, like the trope of an undertaker. He even wore the requisite black suit. He had been particularly cruel to the children. When he was around, Tommy would hide beneath a table.

Later in the evening during our first visit, the curator handed Tonya a carved wood cudgel, about two and a half feet long, without offering any information. Right away, she knew to whom it belonged. Like an Irish beat cop walking the streets of turn-of-the-century New York with his nightstick, the superintendent would rotate the cudgel in his hand as he walked the hallways and hit the children he passed with it, whether they had been misbehaving or not.

In between our two visits to the museum, we did a presentation in the area about our experiences with the paranormal. One of the pictures in our slide show was of a Man in Black whose features were those of a gaunt figure with sunken eyes. After the presentation, a grandmother brought her ten-year-old granddaughter to see us at our display table. She had said to her grandmother when the slide came up, "That's the bad man from the museum."

The grandmother also told us that they had smelled curry, as well as lavender, in the women's bathroom.

In a certain room off one of the building's long hallways, board members and others have reported hearing noises when they are outside it, but when they enter, it stops.

There is also a fancy antique chair that holds the residual haunting of a woman in Victorian-era lace-up boots. If someone sits in the chair (as Tonya did) they can see a woman in a full skirt from the same era who is attached to an "heirloom" in the room opposite the chair. Going into the room, Tonya heard the woman's name (Margaret) and that what she is attached to is a butter churn that was central to her family's life and had been for generations.

Within the museum is the re-creation of a former local general store, complete with the counter, cash register, and some of the items that had been for sale. There is also a turn-of-the-century bicycle, the type with an oversized front tire. Tonya saw what the curator confirmed was the store's owner after she described him as having light brown hair and wearing a blue gingham shirt and straw hat. He was very friendly and happy to have us in his store. So much so that, after we left the room, he summoned us back for a second perusal of his wares.

While we were in that room, Joey had an experience that is rare for him. Looking out the window at a field down a short slope, he saw three spectral Native Americans dancing between two trees. He did not see them in his mind's eye. They were actually there, ephemeral though they were, dancing and chanting.

Going outside, Tonya and another researcher confirmed that this was a ceremonial spot. Tonya could see a spectral fire at the top of a ceremonial circle.

The relationship of that area to Native Americans is bloody and complex and could account for many of the human and nonhuman sightings reported there. There is even a rumor that there are bodies beneath a pavilion on the property. Bodies that had been "relocated" more than once as the area had seen an increase in shopping malls and other suburban sprawl. Tonya could hear wailing in that area.

As we arrived for our second visit, the Mennonite by the orchard was again present. There was also a woman in a white dress on the front porch. This can be a positive sign that the ghosts and spirits in residence are welcoming you into their space.

We had several things that we wanted to accomplish during our second visit. First, however, we were invited to take part in a clearing and blessing ceremony near to where we saw the Native Americans. The ceremony had several parts, and half a dozen sensitives and psychics were in attendance who were well practiced in these types of rituals. We also contributed herbs and prayers from our own training in various spiritual systems. We were not surprised when we all began to experience a number of different phenomena, including a red-brown mass that emerged from the tree line, which Joey saw morph into a rod shape in the sky.

As we flooded the area with white light, Joey got a strong sense that the ghost of the superintendent was becoming very angry and starting to pace in the upstairs of the museum. Someone else, without Joey saying what he was sensing, heard a door slam shut. Joey could also sense the little boy named Tommy was hiding under the Boy Scout badge display case.

After the ceremony, we moved to a tree where several men had been hung during a dark time in the county's history. The energy at the tree was sharp. Joey felt like he was going to throw up. We all joined our intention to clear the energy from the tree. Afterward, except for the very center of the tree, which was still electromagnetically active, the energy through most of it and in the surrounding area was much better. Perhaps some of the ghosts associated with it had crossed over.

An interesting synchronicity, or perhaps irony, of this "hanging tree" was that, at some point in its development, someone had lashed together two of its large limbs with a chain. Over time, the chain had grown into the wood and was actually killing it. In effect, the tree itself had been "hung."

Given the superintendent's anger at the clearing and blessing ceremony, Joey, the curator, and another investigative team member decided it was best to go upstairs before the rest of the investigators entered the building. Using his dowsing rods, the investigator got confirmation from one of his nonhuman spirit contacts in the museum that the superintendent was so angry he had left. The little boy, Tommy, was still hiding, however. Once Tonya came upstairs Tommy's mood improved and he began running around, excited to see her. Tonya also learned that he is friends with the woman named Margaret whose family owned the butter churn.

Through an interesting synchronicity, we found out what Tommy looks like. Joey was walking past an oval portrait upstairs when he heard a voice in his head say, "That's Tommy." When he caught up with Tonya later, she said, "I found a portrait of Tommy." It was the same one.

As he was snapping photos of equipment and vintage books for one of his writing projects, Joey got an EVP of a man laughing in the room where all of the doctor's instruments and supplies are displayed. The tone of the laugh is not at all sinister. It is likely that whomever they belonged to, he was very happy that Joey had taken an interest in them.

One of the tasks on our list was to cross over the Indian woman in the bathroom. Tonya took two other psychics into the bathroom with her. She found out that the woman was an indentured servant who missed home and her family and was confused about where she was. With help from one of our deceased mentors, the three psychics were successful in crossing the woman over.

We also learned during that visit that the puppets that are often moved in the display cabinet are adjusted by their former caretaker.

This historical museum holds many mysteries. It could support a book all its own. In spring of 2020, the curator invited us to lead a special investigation there but he had to cancel it due to COVID-19. We hope to continue to report on this very special haunted facility and its grounds in future books, during *Into the Outer Realms*, and during radio and other appearances.

Hurt Feelings in a Family Cemetery

Although cemeteries are one of the first places we think of when we think about hauntings, most that we have encountered have been quiet, peaceful places, although there have been a few exceptions.

When our daughter Jolie, who is a talented psychic medium, was four years old, we visited a post–Civil War cemetery in Arkansas that had also been a battlefield. As we were looking for family names on the grave markers, Jolie became excited, shouting about "Ghostesses!" coming from the tree line. She also heard drumming, which Tonya confirmed. Jolie then began to describe the soldiers, whom she said were quickly approaching. When she urged us to leave, we of course agreed.

As we mentioned in Part I, the Old Burial Ground in Beaufort, North Carolina, which has been there since the mid-1720s, was another very active site that we encountered. We lived a quarter a mile from it for three years, and walked past it every day and visited it at least once a week. It is a feature of the Beaufort Ghost Walk, where costumed tour guides tell stories of the privateer Otway Burns, a little girl's grave that was broken into by robbers in the 1800s and now has a permanent light fixture over it because she was scared of the dark, and the Little Rum Girl, who died of the plague during trans-Atlantic passage in the late 1700s and was kept in a barrel of rum for the journey home and then buried in it. Her gravesite is filled with toys and trinkets that visitors leave. She also appears to little children as a playful girl but to adults she often appears as an angry, frightening spirit.

We also had dreams about graves that later turned out to be there, just as we dreamed them, and we saw various ghosts and spirits over the years. One night, as we were walking past its wrought iron gates, we heard phantom footsteps behind us. We also had a few encounters there with nonhuman entities.

We recently helped a grieving mother find some peace when Tonya was able to communicate with her daughter, murdered at nineteen after falling into opioid addiction after being prescribed painkillers for back surgery when she was sixteen years old. The daughter had first come through for Tonya the year before during a reading she was doing for the mother.

Later that year, we were approached by Sam Graber, a longtime collaborator of Joey's in theatre education and now a popular podcaster, about being the central story on an episode titled "Ghosted" on his monthly podcast, *American Refugee*.

In February 2020, Sam traveled in from Minneapolis and the mother from California for the investigation. It happened to fall on her birthday, which we do not believe was a coincidence. We made contact with the daughter in several places that evening, including the secluded country road where passersby had found her naked, beaten body. We were surprised to learn that this site is only two miles from our house! Tonya had actually met the mother and done the initial reading for her 40 minutes away, at a spiritual center where Tonya worked a few days a week.

Those are two synchronicities indicating that a higher power, or perhaps the daughter herself, had engineered our help with resolving her murder and giving her mother some peace.

At her gravesite we had communication from not only her (she was in her soccer uniform, kicking a ball and smiling) but from several others, including the mother's murdered father. It is important to note that the daughter indicated that her soul had left her body before it was left on the side of the road and she felt no attachment to that place or what had happened to her.

When Joey downloaded the digital recordings we made that night there were distinct communications (some as simple as "Hello" or "Hi there") from at least a dozen ghosts and spirits. As we complete this book, the podcast episode has aired, we have received new information from the daughter about those who killed her and why, and her mother is considering going to the police with a request to reopen the case based on our communications that evening and in the more recent follow-up communications.

The cemetery that gives this section its name is the family plot of a colleague. Some of the graves date back hundreds of years.

When he asked us to bring our equipment and see if we could make contact with any of his relatives we jumped at the chance. The plot is located in beautiful country in the hills of Pennsylvania. A giant oak tree sits in the center of the plot, offering shade to the inhabitants of the few dozen graves.

While we did not make contact with any of his relatives, there was a grave off by itself, to which Joey was drawn. On the P-SB11 we heard snippets of the same song two times, ten minutes apart, which sounded as though it was from the Depression era. Also through the P-SB11, we heard "Hello" spoken twice by a friendly male voice with a slight drawl. We walked over to the grave and made contact with the man buried there, whose name is William. Joey asked our colleague about William's relationship to the family and why he is buried off by himself at the very edge of the fencing. As our colleague told us the story, the temperature light on the P-SB11 turned on several times, indicating affirmative answers. William had worked for the family for a long time. He had a drinking problem, which he confined to the evenings, but was otherwise reliable and valued as a skilled, hard-working employee. It was clear from what Tonya was seeing and the communications we were getting that he was saddened that the family chose to bury him at the very edge of the plot, all by himself. Our colleague shared that he had been arguing with the family genealogists for a long time about the fact that he was completely absent from the family records. William was pleased that we were paying attention to him. A few days after the investigation, our colleague sent us a photo of William and it was a match to whom Tonya was seeing.

We found out several months later that our colleague had brought us to the gravesite because he was considering working with us more closely and he wanted his grandmother, a no-nonsense woman of few words also buried there, to assess us for him.

We were very happy to hear (during one of our live broadcasts on which he was a guest no less) that we had passed the test.

Discovery of a Murder at a Drive-In

In 2019, the owners of a drive-in theater contacted us because they and their staff were experiencing strange goings-on.

The couple had owned the theater since 2007; the wife had worked there since 1999, and the husband had become the manager in 2001.

The wife remembered starting to experience a strange feeling of something watching her beginning around the time they bought the drive-in, although she had never noticed such a sensation prior. At that time, her husband had taken a long-term contract overseas and during his time away things were always breaking. Film wrapped around the back platter of the projection machine, which the couple assured us is almost impossible to do. The wife began to develop the very distinct feeling that someone, or something, in the theater did not like her.

Concession staff began reporting seeing a young woman, who appeared to be screaming in the kitchen from the periphery of their vision.

We headed over to the drive-in on a warm November evening. As soon as we walked into the concession building, Tonya was able to make contact with the young woman, who led Tonya to the kitchen in the rear of the building. Tonya had no idea where she was going; she was simply following the young woman and her intuition. The owners were amazed when Tonya walked immediately to the location where the staff had reported seeing the young woman.

Tonya described the young woman as being in her thirties and wearing a dress that Tonya estimated to be from the late 1940s to early 1950s. The woman shared that her name was Anna. After sharing her name, she led Tonya outside to an area just beyond where the cars pull in to view the movies and showed her a vision of a car from the 1940s, with long fins, parking and dumping her body in the field, which in the vision was remote and empty. Tonya sensed that the woman's body was never found, and that the truth about her disappearance had never been discovered. The husband stated that he and a coworker had heard screams coming from that area of the property.

After showing Tonya the vision from the field, Anna began walking back toward the concession building and shared that while she loved being at the drive-in (she loved movies), she desperately wanted to be noticed and acknowledged. That is why she broke things. Once inside the building, Tonya asked Anna if she was ready to cross over and she agreed. Tonya envisioned a white pillar of light and called on Archangel Michael to assist Anna into it. Tonya's sense of it was that Anna was able to find the peace she needed in order to move on, knowing that now there were others who knew about her death.

The next day, Joey did some online research and could not find a murder, missing person, or cold case linked to the town or county where the drive-in is located. The owners told us that it was built in 1946 and prior to the drive-in the property was a farm.

It is always helpful when you can find old newspaper articles or other historic documents to corroborate information obtained during an investigation; however, it is not always possible. We speculated that the woman might have gone missing from a location far from where the murderer left her body, and because it was Tonya's sense that her body had never been found, local papers would not have reported on it.

This tragedy reminds us of the case we were involved in for the podcast *American Refugee*. And the tale of a murdered girl seeking justice from the Other Side is often used as the central arc in many books that are made into films, from Peter Straub's *Ghost Story* to Richard Matheson's *Stir of Echoes*.

We followed up with the owners of the drive-in shortly after our investigation and were pleased to learn that all was quiet and well since Anna had crossed over.

Part IV: Practical Matters: What to Do When Your Home Is Being Haunted

Catch the Haunting Early

We hope that we have made it more than clear in all of the text that has come before this final section that acting early on in a haunting is your best option for preventing harm to you, your roommates—living and dead—and your home.

Eliminate Mundane Causes for Phenomena

We spend a considerable amount of time—thankfully so—identifying everyday, non-entity causes for what people think are paranormal phenomena.

When you think there may be a haunting in your home, the first step should be to apply our CAP philosophy: *Conditional Anomalous Phenomena*. At this point, be the skeptic that we always endeavor to be. Try to debunk everything that you are experiencing. You can easily test doors, HVAC systems and fans, creaky architecture, tricks of light, and malfunctions of technology that are due to bad wiring, failing batteries, and the like. Woodpeckers, bats, rodents, and other creatures can be the source of scratching and knocking. Someone all too human might even be having (what they consider) some "harmless fun" with you.

If you have eliminated all of the mundane answers, then it is time to use all of the tools in the skeptic's toolbox.

Use Your Intuition

Remember what Tonya always says: *Your body is the best instrument there is*. If your instincts are telling you that the energy in your home has changed, or you hear or see something that truly cannot be explained as something mundane, the worst thing you can do is ignore it. Using the tools in your skeptic's toolbox that we have talked about throughout this book and now go over in detail, try to ascertain what is going on. Take pictures, run a video or security camera, measure the energy and temperature in the active areas of your home, attempt communication, and if you are at all unsure about what is going on and if it might be dangerous, call on your guides and guardian angels and, if necessary, bring in a professional.

As you proceed, be sure to gather data from those around you—both the living and the dead.

Pay Attention to the Behavior of Pets and Children

We have learned to ask clients about their pets and their children when we are doing an intake interview. In the section "A Dangerous Case in Pennsylvania," the reactions of the cats—both the client's descriptions and what we saw ourselves during the site visit—and our short conversation with the grandson yielded data that helped to bring the haunting to an end.

Just before Joey was writing this section, he had a video conference with a colleague who thanked him for helping him resolve a haunting through advice he gave during an episode of *Into the Outer Realms* in which we discussed the easy fix of covering mirrors. Our colleague did so in his bedroom, where his dog was constantly looking at the mirror at night and becoming agitated, and the dog began behaving normally.

There is a story in *Watch Out for the Hallway* about a dog who became the victim of a haunted Eisenhower silver dollar that apported one evening near one of our guests. Tonya gave the coin to the woman and she took it home with her. Weeks later, we received an email. In whatever room in her home the coin was in, the dog behaved strangely and agitated. Once the woman's husband had removed the coin, by taking it to the local bank, the behavior stopped.

During our time living in the house in Tinton Falls, New Jersey, our roommate's cat would be sitting quietly in the living room, when, out of nowhere, he would suddenly screech as if in pain and dart out of the room like a rocket.

So, if your dog or cat stares at seemingly nothing, or barks, meows, or gets aggressive with what appears to be nothing, chances are good that they are seeing an entity.

Use that early warning system to best advantage, as they are also, like children, the ones who suffer most when a haunting escalates beyond manifestation.

In the case of listening to children, we feel so strongly about this that it is the subject of a future book we are writing. We learn by example and our parents and teachers often dismissing what children see as "imaginary friends" or their "overactive imaginations" has created an unfortunate cycle that we would like to end. From memories of past lives to witnessing haunting phenomena and entities, children are often telling the truth and are indeed seeing what they say they are. It is a mistake to dismiss what your children are telling you out of hand, assuming they are making it up. Some of the most vicious attacks and lasting traumas perpetrated by dark entities (such as shadow people) are on children. In addition, when you are trying to manage or eliminate a haunting, the data gleaned from their descriptions could be invaluable to your success.

Although our three children had plenty of experiences throughout our very haunted life, as you have read, and we were careful to honor what they said, our experiences in the Webb Memorial Library taught us a great deal more about just how accurate children can be when describing entities. We learned that many children visiting the Webb would ask to take their "friends" home with them and even identify them by name.

We not only corroborated that there were several children in the Webb—especially in the Children's Room—but that some of the names the living children used correlated to communications we received during our investigation.

The five-year-old boy at the Webb who was seeing Robert (the "man on fire") fortunately had a mother who trusted what her son was seeing.

Teenagers are especially vulnerable to attack by dark entities. Experts have linked puberty with poltergeist activity because of the oftentimes uneven and increased energy patterns at that time in a person's development. We were amazed at how psychic teenage girls suddenly became in the active paranormal battery that is the Webb Memorial Library.

Here is a tip from experience: children and teenagers will often draw what they see as a way of processing it. This is not just a horror movie trope. Jolie produced many drawings of entities that were haunting our homes and we have corroborated some of the things she saw by other means, like the spider-like girl crawling on the ceiling in our Ohio home. We were also able to ease the minds of two very concerned parents a few years ago when they visited our table after we had given a lecture at a conference. Their teen daughter was filling sketchpads with entities she was seeing. Just knowing that their daughter was not mentally ill or acting out for attention, and that they had not somehow failed as parents was a huge relief to them. This was apparent not only in their faces but in their body posture and proximity to each other as a family when they walked away, with the daughter walking between her parents instead of a few feet behind.

Getting Outside Help

You are never in this alone. As many of our colleagues say, you ultimately have power over the entities you encounter, if you know how to use it. Should you feel like you are being intruded upon or attacked and that the haunting is in the Infestation or Oppression phase, call immediately on your spirit guides or angels.

Ours have been invaluable, both when dealing with hauntings in our homes and when helping clients. We have at times felt the energy in the space clear within seconds of our calling on these powerful helpers.

Should you need additional help, then it is time to contact investigators, healers, energy workers, shamans, psychic mediums, and, in the most extreme cases, demonologists/exorcists (who are not all affiliated with the Catholic church; some are ministers or lay people who have completed the proper training).

Revisiting the Four Stages of a Haunting

If at all possible, you want to keep things at the *manifestation* stage, because, once you move even one level up, to *infestation*, there is disruption to your peace of mind, routine, sleep habits, and a persistent feeling that you are not safe in your own space. At this level, you are increasingly vulnerable, which is exactly what dark entities need to take it to *oppression*. Sleep deprivation and constantly having to be on high alert will make you irritable, fearful, and stressed out—a trio of emotional liabilities that will hurt your mental and physical health over time. These are also the main ingredients of the rich energy feast dark entities are trying to obtain at your expense through their manifestation, infestation, and oppression. The final level, *possession*, dwells in the realm of such crisis and danger that desperate measures, such as exorcisms, are often called for.

Thankfully, possession is rare and, although we have chosen not to share any of our experiences with it in this book, we hope that even the thought of this level of haunting is alarming enough to you that it serves as a reminder to act early using the tools we are providing.

What's the Story?

Once you and those you call on for help start collecting data, you want to get to work puzzling out the narrative. Knowing the story that the entities are attempting to tell through the haunting is crucial to solve the problem as quickly and peacefully as possible.

Despite what the movies and TV "reality" shows want you to believe, most stories involved with hauntings are not *horror* stories. They are stories of disembodied former humans who have, to use storytelling terms, Wants, Needs, and Motivations that are not that different from our own. Once we know what those are, we are well on the way to solving the mystery and ending the haunting in a peaceful way for both the living and the dead.

As a professional storyteller, story analyst, and teacher, Joey uses what he calls the *Three 3s of Good Storytelling*, which easily apply to identifying the major components of a haunting.

The first three are probably familiar to you. They are the Who, Where, and What. *Who* is haunting? *Who* is being haunted? *Where* is the haunting taking place? *What* is the Main Problem? In other words, *what* are the Wants, Needs, and Motivations not being met or acknowledged?

With regard to the What, begin by identifying what was happening when the Manifestation began. Here are some easy questions to ask:

What has changed in your life or home?

Has there been an unusual or increased level of family tension and conflict?

Has anyone in the home undergone a recent trauma or had an old one resurface?

Has someone new moved in, or have they been staying with you for a long period of time?

Has your family suffered a recent loss of someone close to them? Have the prior occupants?

Have any new objects been purchased, especially antiques?

Have you been to a haunted location or remote area (such as the woods or a cave) where you might have picked up an entity that followed you back?

Has there been a change in your sleep or dream patterns?

Are you in a new home?

Have any renovations or new construction been done to the home, by you or prior to your moving in?

What is the history of your home and neighborhood? (Neighborhoods can be haunted too!)

Before you buy a home, especially if any of the potential occupants are sensitives, research what the disclosure policies are for any deaths, crimes, or hauntings. They vary by state. But, if you ask about these things, the real estate agent should have to answer honestly. Above all, trust your gut. Your intuition. If the energy or atmosphere feels uncomfortable in the house, trust that as reason enough to walk away and find something else.

The second part of the Three 3s is the Beginning, Middle, and End. For most hauntings, our goal for both our clients and for you is that both the beginning and the end are contained in the *manifestation* phase and the middle (where you overcome obstacles to solve the Main Problem) consists of your successful application of the strategies in this book.

The third part of the Three 3s is Circumstances, Conflict, and Climax. Since Circumstances are the most complex, we are going to leave them for last. If possible, we want to avoid Conflict with ghosts, spirits, and other entities. This is where negotiation and the setting of boundaries and following the Paranormal Bill of Rights are of greatest value. We also want the Climax to be a peaceful resolution, meaning agreed-on cohabitation or the crossing over or other peaceful removal of the entity. What we do not want is some of the more tense, violent, and disruptive conflicts and climaxes that you have read about in the cases we have shared and that you see on TV and in the cinema.

In Joey's thirty years as a professional writer, story analyst, and teacher, he has developed ways for writers and students to make sense of the often difficult-to-master rules and techniques for creating a compelling story. For Circumstances he decided on the following formula:

Circumstances = How the Where + the What (Main Problem) affect the Who's (Character's) behavior.

This works very well when we consider what happens during Manifestation, Infestation, Oppression, and Possession. The worse the phenomena (the Problem) at the site of the haunting (the Where), the more they will affect the (living or dead) Character's behavior.

A Case Study Applying the Three 3s

To demonstrate how this can be of practical value in identifying the substance of a haunting, we have chosen to break down the case study we call "Generations of Hauntings in a Multi-Family Victorian" using the Three 3s.

The Basics

<u>Who</u>: *The Living*: The husband and wife who own the house and their daughter and her three children. *The Deceased*: Two of the previous owners (one male, one female) and a woman attached to the fireplace, which the current owners repurposed from a house that had a fire.

<u>Where</u>: An old Victorian, and the property on which it sits, that has undergone numerous renovations over the years, whose ownership was at times contested, leading to a fierce sense of possession and protection of it by some of the deceased former occupants. It is situated in an area of rural Pennsylvania known for its hauntings and paranormal phenomena.

<u>What/The Problem(s)</u>: The man and woman who had each previously owned the house were disrupting the family, including sleep disruption, physical harm, and poltergeist activity, after the daughter and three children moved in with most of their belongings.

The Framework
Beginning: The daughter and her children move in with most of their belongings during a time of personal crisis.
Middle: Sleep issues, things thrown, people pushed down stairs, noises, strange lights, things moved and broken.
End: Crossed the female former occupant over; blessed the house and warded the property; set boundaries with the deceased male owner.

The Mechanics
Circumstances: For the *deceased*, the circumstances changed when the daughter and her three children moved in, bringing many of their belongings and occupying bedrooms previously empty. For the *living*, the angry responses of the deceased caused sleep deprivation, stress, anxiety, and daily disruption, adding to an already difficult familial situation.
Conflict: For the *living*, there was physical as well as emotional harm and one of the boys was in a sleep study and on medication because of the sleep disruption caused by the female ghost with dementia. The occupants of the house did not feel safe. For the *deceased*, the additional occupants, furniture, boxes, and so on and the loss of areas of the house that they had claimed upset them.
Climax: Our initial warding of the property escalated some of the activity in the home. Our crossing over the woman with dementia and setting boundaries with the original owner and blessing the house ended the phenomena and brought the situation from Oppression back to Manifestation.

Strategies for Managing or Ending a Haunting

Respect

Once you have some details, it is time to address the issue head on. First and foremost, however, approach any attempt to engage with and manage a haunting with *respect*. Always keep our Paranormal Bill of Rights handy as a reminder. Not only are you requesting respect from whatever it is that is creating the haunting—you must also respect them. Even in the case of a dark entity, there must be a level of respect for the seriousness of the situation and the dangerous capabilities of such an entity. We are speaking here about the same level of respect we show for a powerful lightning storm or a storm at sea.

Intention

Along with respect, there is intention. Know exactly why you are doing what you are doing. Know what you want from the situation. This is good practice for a well-lived life outside of managing or ending a haunting. You cannot communicate your wants and needs and set boundaries if you do not have clear intention. We have designed, based on over a decade of training and experience, or gathered from reputable, tried and true sources the tools in this book to help you with clarity in your attention and intention. Do you want to cohabitate with the entity or entities? Do you want to help them in some way to fulfill their Wants, Needs, and Motivations? Do you want to cross them over or otherwise have them removed from the space? Clear intention is the pathway to clear communication. Do not attempt to resolve or manage the haunting until your intention is clear.

When it is appropriate, power your intention with positive energy, positive thoughts, and laughter. Having a sense of humor during a manifestation has been invaluable to us and it keeps the energy-feast of fear from emerging. Remember—the energy of fear is what dark entities want. Conversely, many ghosts and spirits have a wonderful sense of humor and will also appreciate yours.

It is important to say that, when we say laughter, we do not mean *laughing at* an entity. That is mockery, which goes against not only the tenets of the Paranormal Bill of Rights but shows a marked lack of respect. How readily will you negotiate with or respect the boundaries of someone who is laughing at you? Most likely, quite the opposite will happen, leading to a quick and nasty escalation.

The Three 3s exercise and your research should provide the information necessary to formulate a clear intention.

Protecting, Clearing, and Warding Your Home

If you want your home to be a place of tranquility, peace, and positive manifestation, do not wait for it to be haunted to protect or clear it. Even better than early intervention is taking preventative measures. In the following sections, we share some of our favorite tools for protecting and clearing the home. They are our favorites because they are most effective, but we also have sensory preferences, as will you. With tools like essential oils and incense, each has its own properties, which you will want to research, although you may be put off by certain smells of the prescribed remedy. In almost all cases, there are substitutes that will work just as well for the particular issue you are trying to resolve. Trust your intuition when choosing the right tools for you.

As Tonya writes about in detail in *Living the Intuitive Life*, protecting your energetic and physical bodies is just as important as protecting your living space. As you are protecting and cleansing your home, practices such as yoga, deep breathing, and meditation will raise your energy vibration and frequency, which wards off dark entities and prevents them from getting the energy feast they so desperately crave.

Plus, it is an excellent practice for having a life well lived.

Essential Oils. Essential oils are naturally occurring, vaporizing, aromatic compounds found in plants, which they protect and help with pollination. Essential oils have applications in beauty treatments, food preparation and preservation, and for healing. Essential oils have the highest vibrational frequencies of any natural substance on Earth, and resonate with the electrical field of a healthy human body.

Essential oils also have a variety of ways that you can interact with them: you can inhale them, use them topically, and diffuse them. Diffusers are designed specifically to break essential oils into small particles and disperse them into the air. Each oil has its recommended uses and delivery mechanisms, so be sure to do your research. Basil, for instance, can be an irritant to your nasal passages and eyes when diffused, as can pine.

We highly recommend diffusing oils in a room where a haunting is taking place. We also do it as a matter of daily practice in active areas of our home.

Some oils that provide not only excellent energetic support but also are effective in protecting or clearing your home are rosemary, frankincense, sandalwood, and myrrh.

Essential oils are not regulated by regulatory agencies such as the Food and Drug Administration, so it is important to buy from certified companies who provide only pure, *therapeutic grade* oils.

Sage. Chances are, of all the tools for protection and cleansing, you are most familiar with sage. Sage is used on all of the paranormal investigation shows as a remedy for hauntings, and with good reason. For centuries, sage has proven to be highly effective in clearing away negative energies, including fear and anger. Indigenous peoples use sage bundles (or smudge sticks) at both the start of and during their rituals—a process called "smudging." Sage bundles are easy to get on both the Internet and at metaphysical stores. Some people do not like the smell of sage. It can be pungent and linger for quite a while after you burn it. If you find you dislike the smell, we suggest using the sage and then leaving the home for a little while to let it clear.

This little inconvenience is worth it.

Backing up and adding to the positive spiritual benefits of sage, scientific research shows that its smoke clears bacteria, including staphylococcus, out of the air; these antibacterial benefits last
for quite some time after the smoke clears.

As you have probably seen on television, the most efficient method of using a sage bundle is to have a bowl or large seashell beneath the lit bundle to catch the falling ash. As you light it, state your *intention*. Be clear and firm, but state it with peace and gratitude. Smudge the home, moving in a clockwise motion, going from room to room, and the people in it, including yourself. You can use your hand or a feather to disperse the smoke. When you are smudging people, let them wave the smoke toward themselves. The hand or feather method will also keep the sage bundle lit.

Saying a prayer or mantra as you move through your home is an excellent way to reinforce your intention during the smudging ritual. The prayer to St. Michael the Archangel is a powerful addition to this practice in the case of a dark, malevolent entity, and goes as follows: "St. Michael the Archangel defend us in battle, be our protection against the wickedness and snares of the devil. May God rebuke him we humbly pray; and do thou, O Prince of the Heavenly host, by the power of God, cast into hell Satan and all the evil spirits who prowl about the world seeking the ruin of souls. Amen." Regardless of religious affiliation or background, we have found this prayer to be extremely effective. People worldwide have reported accounts of assistance from Michael and his angels; however, any prayer or mantra that elicits a sense of faith and empowerment for you will serve to reinforce your intention for clearing and protection.

Gently pressing the lit end of the bundle into the bowl or seashell is typically enough to extinguish it. You could also put it into a bowl of damp sand.

When we are not using our sage bundle, we keep it in the seashell covered with a blessed cloth or red felt to honor its healing and protective properties.

Frankincense resin. If you want a little more power and smoke in clearing a space, we suggest Frankincense resin. These are small crystals that you place on a specially designed "puck" of heated charcoal. Clergy use Frankincense resin for Roman Catholic mass, especially High Holy days. When Joey was a boy he had to leave the church when the priest was swinging the censer that dispersed the resin smoke because it made him gag, but he now has become accustomed to and even enjoys the smell of the smoke. And it leaves a room energetically charged in a positive, peaceful way.

Incense. Like the smoke from sage, incense smoke is both cleansing and purifying, and for thousands of years it has been an integral part of the ritual cleansing and purification of sacred spaces. For added meaning, envision the smoke rising upward beyond the space you are in, carrying your intentions and prayers to a Higher Source. The act of lighting the incense while vocalizing your intention and then watching it drift skyward aligns your frequency with the positive results you desire. Some spiritual practices necessitate cracking a window to allow the smoke to travel outside the home; however, it is probable that this gesture is more symbolic than literal.

As with essential oils, there are countless varieties of incense and there are considerable differences in quality. It is worth spending a few more dollars to avoid the dollar-a-box incense in the home furnishings section in the typical box store, which has additives and artificial perfumes that make it burn more quickly and can trigger allergy-like symptoms in some people.

We recommend Nag Champa, although there are several other quality brands.

Like the frankincense used in the Catholic mass in resin form since the eleventh century, Frankincense in incense form has antiseptic and disinfectant properties without the intensity of smoke and smell.

Although incense is usually set into a sled or bowl for burning, you can use it the same way as a smudge stick to cleanse away negative energies in a particular area.

We light incense throughout the day, in whatever room we are in, and always before and during prayer, ritual, or meditation. We also use a combination of essential oils, sage, and incense to cleanse and protect our bedroom each night before we sleep.

Epsom salts and Dead Sea salt. For centuries, healers and spiritual practitioners have understood the neutralizing benefits of salt. It is widely used for removing negativity. After we have completed an investigation or even when we have been in a crowded store full of rushing, agitated people, we bathe or shower using Epsom salt. For a bath, simply pour a handful beneath the open faucet as you are filling the tub. We also sometimes add a few drops of our favorite essential oils. If you prefer, you can also purchase Epsom salts with oils added, such as lavender. For a shower, put a small amount of salt into your hands and rub it into your skin. In addition to clearing the energetic field, it is an excellent exfoliate.

During one particularly tense night at the Webb Library, after dealing with some dark and difficult entities, we did not wait to return home to take advantage of Epsom salts' healing properties. We drove the few blocks to the ocean and waded in up to our knees.

Dead Sea salt is a little more costly, but equally effective in removing negative energies.

Regardless of which type you choose, keep the bath or shower to twenty minutes, as that is the acknowledged point at which the salts are no longer effective.

Bells and chimes. The more you approach the cleansing and protection of your home or other personal space like a ritual, the more focused will be your intention. Another tool to signal that you are undertaking a ritual is to use the healing sounds and vibrations of bells and chimes. The vibration of ringing bells breaks up negative and stagnant energy. Bells and chimes also leave a crystal-clear energy field in the space in which you use them. The frequency of this energy will depend on the size of the bell or chime and the type of material used to cast it. As with all of the tools in this section, quality varies. There are a wide variety available, with different motifs and decorations. A metaphysical brick and mortar or online store is a good place to start.

Clearing a space using sound is as simple as ringing your bell or chime. You can also use a Tibetan singing bowl. You will be able to tell that the energy has improved because the tone from the bell or chime will sound much clearer and last much longer as you work to clear the space. Keeping in mind the goal of performing a ritual, you can strike the bell or chime three times, a number that we are taught has special power from writings, both nonfiction and fiction, throughout the ages.

As with salts, striking a bell or chime can clear your energetic body after an investigation and even send away any entities that might have attached to you and followed you home.

If you do not have access to a bell or chimes, you can use recordings, readily available online, of the tones that they produce.

Crystals and gemstones. Crystals and gemstones transmute and magnify various

energies. Quartz crystal is widely used in electronic devices because of its conductivity. Quartz is the most common form of crystal on Earth, and its variety of colors include rose quartz, smoky quartz, amethyst, and citrine. Natural quartz deposits often correlate with paranormal hotspots. Crystals that clear negative energies include amethyst, obsidian, clear quartz, rose quartz, smoky quartz, and lapis lazuli. There are also others.

When choosing crystals and gemstones, use your intuition. With your eyes closed, hold them

in your hand and "listen" to how each one affects your body. You can use a pendulum, dowsing rods, or any of the "muscle testing" techniques to determine which are best for you.

We take our amethyst and quartz crystals for protection when we do investigations. Joey is never without his black tourmaline and tiger's eye. When Tonya gives psychic readings, she makes sure to have nearby the oval lapis stone gifted to her by one of her spirit guides.

Periodically, you need to cleanse your crystals and gemstones from accumulated negative energies by placing them for a few hours in direct sunlight or moonlight. Placing them in a bag of salt for a few hours also works well, as does smudging them with sage.

Other herbs and tools to burn or offer for cleansing and protection. For cleansing, protection, and ritual and ceremony in our home, we always keep on hand a supply of palo santo, tobacco, and rosemary. We also have them in our field bags for investigations and home clearings and warding. Palo santo is a fragrant wood. We use tobacco in the Native American tradition as an offering to guides and spirits. Rosemary symbolizes remembrance and good fortune. When we are preparing to cross over a ghost, Joey uses a combination of all three in his preparation. You can read about our applications of these tools in the cases in this book.

Visualization. One of the most powerful tools there is for protecting and clearing your home is your own imagination. Visualization is a tool to focus your imagination. One of Joey's college acting professors likened it to bringing a sunbeam down to a laser beam. This goes hand in glove with attention, intention, and focus. Neurologists have scientifically proven that visualizing a place, action, or outcome affects cognitive processes in the brain that control motor function, attention, perception, and memory. It even works on the energetic body.

The foundational visualization for this kind of work and practice is to imagine yourself surrounded by white light. This is our first step when undertaking an investigation, ritual, or ceremony. It is as simple as closing your eyes and taking a few deep breaths to quiet your mind. Each time you inhale, imagine a beautiful, bright white light coming in through the crown of your head and surrounding your entire body. Feel the warmth of the light protecting and supporting you. After several breaths, expand the light into a protective bubble around your body. Make it as wide and as bright as you wish it to be.

Recall the ritual we did with several other healers and investigators at the historical society building in Pennsylvania. The ball of light was expansive—encompassing a good bit of the sky. Recall that at least one ghost felt its effect hundreds of feet away, inside the main building, while we were outside.

When using visualization, evoke all five of the senses. When you picture yourself in a place, take in not only the sights, but the sounds, smells, tastes, and how things feel. When you engage with all of your senses, the visualization becomes most lifelike and is most effective. It also works to open up additional sensing systems.

While we were writing this section, we used visualization to clear a troublesome entity by choosing a spot in imaginary woods modeled on those behind our home. It was here that we would undertake the ritual, with the help of our guides. We each had a role to play. Tonya was going to burn and bury the entity and then ward the burial site while Joey and his spirit guides created a protective perimeter. The visualization lasted roughly twenty minutes. When we finished and compared our experiences, we found several specific details not a part of our "script" that we both experienced. We had fully engaged all five senses—Joey could smell the burning of the entity as if it were right next to him—and there were a few unexpected encounters of which both of us were aware.

Visualization is a powerful tool for manifesting what you most desire in your life—including managing or ending a haunting. You can also use it for connecting with your spirit guides and guardian angels.

Prayer. Prayer is, outside of its obvious religious applications, a combination of *intention*, *visualization*, and *recognizing the power of your words*. Research has repeatedly shown the effectiveness of prayer and there are of course millions of believers in its ability to connect with God, the Source, the Universe, or however you choose to name a Higher Power.

Thoughts backed by intention are a powerful form of energy. When you practice prayer with heartfelt intention, you emit energetic signals into your surrounding environment. Tonya's favorite prayer since childhood is The Lord's Prayer. When she was writing *Living the Intuitive Life*, she discovered that Dana Williams had found a correlation between the text of The Lord's Prayer and the seven major chakras and twelve archetypal paths of life. You can learn more about this important overlap in spiritual systems in Marianne Williams's *The Lord's Prayer, the Seven Chakras, the Twelve Life Paths: The Prayer of Christ Consciousness as a Light for the Auric Centers and a Map through the Archetypal Life Paths of Astrology*.

The Lord's Prayer is only one of thousands that spiritual practitioners have written and used over the course of human history. Affirmations and mantras work as well. They are specifically written to evoke "seed sounds" that interact with your chakras. We often write our own prayers for a specific situation and we encourage you to do the same.

One we are using as we write this section to re-ward the property on which we live is:

We ask protection for this property

The house we live in
And the people who live in it.
We ask protection from evil, ill intention, and bad luck.
We ask that Love and Light
Surround this property and home
And protect it from dark forces.

We wrote this prayer to recite while burying iron in the four corners of the property on which we live. We spoke it repeatedly as we poured a perimeter of salt around it during the time that a dark, winged entity was attempting to attach itself to Joey while he was working on a screenplay with paranormal and horror elements, an incident we relate in the section on our home in Leavittsburg, Ohio.

We also used this prayer on the property where the Victorian home sits and the property adjacent to the drive-in, where the owners intend to build a new home.

The Role of Consciousness

There is mounting scientific evidence that consciousness not only survives death but also significantly determines our experience of so-called reality. So we need to be, well... *conscious* all the time of how we are perceiving things and what we are interpreting them to be. This is especially important when engaging with a haunting. We do not want to be guilty of *projection*—assigning labels and assumptions to the haunting based on our own biases and worldviews instead of collecting data, constructing a narrative, and making determinations based on that information and any other data we are collecting in real time while working with the haunting. There may have been a less positive outcome in the house with the shadow people in Pennsylvania, for instance, if we had not wavered from the initial theory that they were djinn. Although, as we have said, there are significant similarities between djinn and shadow people, the differences are there and it pays to be exact.

As we shared in the case of misidentification in Ohio, making your determinations of what is happening based on what you have seen on the "reality shows" and through the lens of your own psychology and past traumas can only lead to misinformation, tension, and misidentification that makes a peaceful resolution all the harder to achieve. Remember—not everything that is angry, mischievous, or even rude or bullying is a demon. We must also account for confusion and frustration on the part of a ghost. As we learned with a ghost named Paul in the Webb Library and the suicide victim who was haunting a client's home in Ohio, a head injury can cause cognitive deficits on the Other Side.

The TV trope of "banishing a demon back to Hell!" is best kept in the realms of fictional stories until the data make it clear that it is indeed a demon or other dark entity with which you are dealing. Even then, respect and humility are a smarter approach than thinking that you are the weapon-brandishing Vanquisher and Savior out a superhero film.

Communication

Second only to seeing or capturing on video or in a photo a full-bodied apparition is the capturing of an EVP, or *electronic voice phenomenon*. Hearing a voice or voices from the Other Side is a rite of passage moment for a paranormal investigator.

Communication with the Other Side is also an essential tool when trying to understand, manage, or end a haunting. Throughout this book, we have shared communications we have received through the *spirit box* (we prefer and recommend the P-SB11) and digital versions of spirit boxes, although we still have not made a complete assessment of these. So far, Ghost Radar seems to be the most reliable, as the words and names that appear on the app are usually relevant to what is actually happening in the moment. A recent example of this happened when Tonya and a friend were investigating a historic hotel in Ohio. Tonya had the Ghost Radar app on when she entered the lobby and looked up at the ceiling, painted with clouds. From a separate part of the lobby ceiling hung an eleven-foot pilot wheel from a steamboat. Moments later, the words "Wheel" and "Clouds" appeared on the Ghost Radar app. Our experience with Necrophonics results have been mixed and vague. These ghost communication apps are helpful when used with a traditional spirit box or other means of communication and less so when used on their own.

When using any of these devices, we recommend also running a *digital tape recorder*. Often communications, true EVPs, appear on the digital recording although we did not hear them in real time, even while wearing a good pair of headphones.

Speaking of, once you have had an EVP session or otherwise run a spirit box, digital or analog, you can then download the digital recording you made into an audio software program (Audacity is free and easy to use). Then comes the tedium of listening through headphones for communications. Since the software displays waveforms, with practice you can see a clear communication on the screen, although voices from the Other Side do not behave and appear visually like human communication, so it is best to listen, second by second. You can delete sections as you go and mark areas to go back and listen to again.

On the recent investigation into the murder of the daughter of someone who asked for our help in getting answers, we recorded, between her gravesite and the spot where passersby found her body in the weeds on a desolate road, well over an hour of the spirit box cycling through its frequencies. Over the course of several hours, Joey isolated thirteen separate voice communications, from almost as many entities, and all combined it was less than 30 seconds of material.

In the past year, we have also used *dowsing rods and pendulums* to communicate with the Other Side. We have learned much about their use through trial and error and have come to consider them a primary tool for communication—even more so than the spirit box. Tonya is writing a book on their use for guidance and during an investigation and we have begun to train others how to use them. Like using a flashlight or EMF meter for communication, you are limited to Yes/No questions, and we have found this to be a benefit. It forces you to be very specific when formulating your questions (which means having a clear intention) and the answers are less open to interpretation than a string of static-carried words about which at times no two people can agree.

A controversial communication device is the *talking or spirit board* (the trademarked parlor game name, Ouija, is the most popular). It takes a practiced individual, protected by white light and very clear on intention, to have success using a talking board. In many cases, low-vibrational entities come through that are tricksters who lure the user in over time, often either pretending at first to be a child, or just taking an outright frightening approach from the start. Using a talking board without proper training and seriousness of intention can quickly lead to Manifestation, Infestation, and so on. Sir Arthur Conan Doyle, one of the grandfathers of paranormal investigation, likened using a talking board to leaving your window open with a candle lit on the sill in the middle of the night in a bad neighborhood. Joey relates a frightening experience he had with a Ouija board when he was sixteen in *Watch Out for the Hallway*. It would be thirty years before he would again place his hands on a planchette, and he only agreed to do so because he was with two very experienced psychic-mediums.

Tonya, as a psychic medium, can communicate with ghosts and spirits without these devices. On rare occasions, Joey has had the ability to hear spirits become active and even speak, the technical term for which is *clairaudience*.

In the ten years of our work as paranormal investigators and even longer as experiencers, we have had every kind of verbal communication imaginable, from funny to sarcastic to frightening. The Webb Library yielded hundreds of communications with the P-SB11 and other devices, including conversations that lasted for six to eight exchanges. We have never had such consistent communication with the P-SB11 anywhere else.

Be specific in the questions you ask. Make sure they are clear and only ask one question at a time (this is another reason why pendulums and dowsing rods are at times preferable). Ask the entities questions with the respect you would give to anyone with whom you wished to communicate and have a productive conversation. It is easy to get frustrated if you are getting no answers, obscure answers, or otherwise not the answers you seek. Keep breathing and remember that tension and hostility will not make for fruitful communication. Do not ask needlessly prying or unnecessary questions. These kinds of questions lead to trickster behavior on the part of the entity. Entities that do not want to either speak to you or become fatigued after a time are capable of responding in misleading ways, draining batteries, jamming the signal, or otherwise rendering the devices nonfunctional. They will also tell you, "No more" or "Enough."

It is essential to respect such a request and put the device away.

Dowsing rods and pendulums are, again, a good place to start because of the Yes/No limitations. For each, surround yourself in white light, be clear why you are using this tool for communication, and then ask for an indication of what is Yes and what is No. For Tonya's dowsing rods, they open up wide for Yes and cross for No. Joey's pendulum swings perfectly back and forth for Yes and rotates counterclockwise for No. The more emphatic the No, the wider the arc.

It is not good practice to use communication devices for speaking with the dead in your home or elsewhere "just for fun." These devices increase paranormal activity. After all, once you call out to the Other Side, it would be silly not to expect plenty of answers. Entities often crave communication and once they answer your call, they might not want to leave.

Setting Boundaries and Negotiation

As we said at the start of the book—only you can judge how much haunting you are able to tolerate. For us, the paranormal and supernatural are such a part of our lives, and we have experienced so much over the past twenty-plus years, that having ghosts and spirits pass through or even take up residence for a time has added to the variety of our lives. We have come to see much of this as *normal* and *natural*. We are able to track a haunting from its early Manifestation and take remedies to keep it from becoming an Infestation—or worse.

If you have taken all of the steps in this final section of the book and the haunting in your home or business is still unmanageable, it is time to step up your efforts to set boundaries and, if it is sensible to do so, negotiate with the spirit(s) or ghost(s) haunting your home.

Quoting the Paranormal Bill of Rights, point 8: *In a case where entities are overstepping their bounds, we talk to them—as you would a partner, neighbor, or coworker—explaining our position and*
asking them to work with us.

In several of our homes and on cases, this simple practice has often brought the haunting to a place of peace, where it remains in the Manifestation phase and no harm is done to the living or the dead. This is our recommendation if the haunting involves someone attached to either the house, the property, or a piece of furniture or architectural feature (such as the fireplace in the Victorian home in

Pennsylvania). We owe a good bit of respect to these former occupants. Their attachments are understandable. If they are not being threatening, causing you undo aggravation, or destroying your property, setting boundaries and perhaps even negotiating is a reasonable request.

In the case of Frank, the original owner of our Ohio home, moving Joey's audio recording equipment out of the space that Frank claimed as his own went a long way in solving the problem of his moving things around in that room. Joey only took that step after trying several times to convince Frank that sharing the space was a reasonable option and using the other tools we share in this section. Joey was lucky to have another room into which to move his audio equipment and it actually worked out better. Tonya, following her intuition that Frank simply wanted acknowledgment, went even further, once we had initially settled the situation, and left food and a drink in the kitchen for him while we ate dinner, and he was eventually gone. It's clear that our managing our frustration, bringing the haunting back from Infestation into Manifestation, and showing Frank respect as the original owner of the home by compromising with him allowed further information to come through. We were then able to apply these data and ultimately pave the way for Frank to let go of his attachment to the house and go on to his higher purpose.

Our daughter Jolie, who recently turned 21, has a knack for negotiation with spirits and ghosts. She has been seeing and hearing them since she was at least four years old. She is firm when they cross boundaries, yet she can also be very welcoming and accommodating. She applies just the right amount of humor. A colleague recently told us that she schedules time for spirits and ghosts. They are not permitted in her space at night or while she is working, but in the mid-afternoon they are more than welcome to visit. Well-known psychic mediums James van Praagh and John Edward do the same.

If you are new to the experience of a haunting and have purchased this book to help you solve a current haunting you are trying to manage, then this may sound a little odd. But we believe that those on the Other Side are an everyday part of our lives and all of the same rules apply. Just as with a visiting relative or an annoying neighbor at a campsite, engage with them early to let them know what you are willing to tolerate and actively manage the situation so that tension and stress do not build up, leading you to be less than the best version of yourself and offering the energy feast some entities need to make the haunting worse.

Eight times out of ten, we have seen setting boundaries and negotiation turn a potentially troublesome haunting into a mutually beneficial experience.

Ending a Haunting in Your Home

If none of the strategies and practices in this final section manage a haunting to your satisfaction and level of comfort, or if the haunting is escalating beyond Manifestation or tolerable Infestation, then it is certainly time to take steps to end the haunting.

If it has reached this point, we strongly suggest getting outside help. There is strength in numbers and you should never attempt to cross over a difficult ghost or otherwise end an escalated haunting on your own. There are professionals who have devoted a good portion of their life to the study of paranormal phenomena and have the practical experience to back it up. If you have an active, strong relationship with your spirit guides or with guardian angels, they will be able to assist you—either to end the haunting or with advice on where to go for the help that you need. Ours have been invaluable to us, as we have shared throughout this book.

When bringing in outside help, such as investigators, healers, energy workers, shamans, priests, psychic-mediums, and, in the most extreme cases, demonologists/exorcists, ask for recommendations, either from people you know or from your local metaphysics store or paranormal investigation team. Call a state team and ask if they know anyone who operates near your home or business. You can reach out to paranormal investigators, such as us, with questions and for guidance. It is part of our daily work and we are happy to help those who contact us. Our information is included at the end of this book.

We would not mention this, except that it comes up more often than you might believe—do not partake of any alcohol prior to an investigation or attempted clearing in your home. Being nervous is understandable, but managing it with alcohol is not the way to go. It only makes you a target and sours the energy of the work the investigators, healers, and so on are coming in to do. There were a few nights during the seventy-five we spent at the Webb Library where guest investigators showed up drunk. Beyond the frustrations of having to deal with intoxicated people, who are often short on manners and lack the ability to follow the rules and respect boundaries, we had very little communication from entities when they were present. They do not want to deal with that any more than do the living.

Find people to help with whom you are comfortable—who put you at ease and are not trying to take advantage of you or the situation. As a litmus test, apply point 10 from the Paranormal Bill of Rights to them: *We do not do or distort this work for attention, financial gain, or to seek power over any entity. We undertake this work with Humility, Harmony, and Love.* They may charge a nominal fee to cover expenses, such as travel or lodging, or they may ask, as we do, to tell your story in their books, podcasts, and presentations. This is a way to have your experience shared to help others. Be wary of television producers who want to come in with cameras and ramp things up before "managing" or "ending" the haunting—this happened to one of our clients before they called us. It is not that these people are unkind, but their priorities are not the same as yours. Also walk away from anyone who is trying to charge exorbitant fees or who wants to do things to your home or in your home that make you uncomfortable. Ask them for testimonials and for a detailed explanation of what they want to do and why. The same applies for those offering advice without knowing the details of the situation. If you call someone for help and, after you tell them you are noticing signs of Manifestation, they start prescribing complicated or inappropriate remedies, that is not someone who is ultimately going to help. And their suggestions just might make things worse.

We make a habit, as you have read, of doing, whenever possible, phone and video interviews prior to visiting a home or business. We have a set of questions that we ask, in a casual and nonthreatening way, based on prior experience and training. The data we collect allow us to determine if there is an actual haunting occurring, if we have the right background and skillsets to be of assistance, and to formulate a game plan and employ the appropriate tools, such as those we have detailed in this final section of the book.

The last thing you want is for those tasked with clearing your home to make a situation worse. It has always been considerably more difficult to go in and undo someone else's mistakes than to handle a case that we are the first investigators to take.

Closing Thoughts

Our homes and businesses are places where we should always feel safe. They should not be spaces where we feel stressed out or where we are suffering—financially, emotionally, or otherwise—because we feel a sense of invasion or threat.

A haunting, like energy, can be positive or negative, depending on the Who, the Where, the What, and the Circumstances. Much of what happens is up to us—how we react, the boundaries that we set, our intentions, and our feelings about the haunting.

No matter what you choose—to share your space with ghosts or spirits or to remove them from that space—please use the tools in this book to ensure a peaceful, pleasant experience.

For your sake and for the sake of those on the Other Side.

And, most importantly, don't ever be afraid to tell your story or ask for help.

Feel free to start with us.

Bibliography

Capra, Fritof. 1975. *The Tao of Physics*. Shambala Publications.

Dyer, Wayne W. 2005. *The Power of Intention*. Hay House.

Guiley, Rosemary Ellen. 2013. *The Djinn Connection*. Visionary Living.

Hagelin, John S., Maxwell V. Rainforth, Kenneth L. C. Cavanaugh, Charles N. Alexander, Susan F. Shatkin, John L. Davies, Anne O. Hughes, Emanuel Ross, and David W. Orme-Johnson. 1999. "Effects of Group Practice of the Transcendental Meditation Program on Preventing Violent Crime in Washington, D.C.: Results of the National Demonstration Project." *Social Indicators Research* 47 (2): 153–201.

Hameroffa, Stuart and Roger Penrose. 2014. "Consciousness in the Universe: A Review of the 'Orch OR' Theory." *Physics of Life Reviews* 11 (1): 39–78.

Hardy, Diane, Mamre Wilson, and Marilyn Collins. 1999. *Beaufort's Old Burying Ground: North Carolina*. Arcadia Publishing.

Jung, Carl. 1960. *Synchronicity: An Acausal Connecting Principle*. Princeton University Press.

Keel, John. 1974, May. "Old Patterns in New Waves." *Saga* magazine.

Talbot, Michael. 1993. *Mysticism and the New Physics*. Penguin Arkana.

Williams, Marianne. 2009. *The Lord's Prayer, the Seven Chakras, the Twelve Life Paths: The Prayer of Christ Consciousness as a Light for the Auric Centers and a Map through the Archetypal Life Paths of Astrology*. Attunement Press.

Our Paranormal Bill of Rights

1. Entities and haunted locations are not specimens or "attractions" to be examined or disturbed at our whim, for our amusement, or to satisfy our curiosity.
2. We ask permission before we enter the space inhabited by an entity or entities.
3. It is not our place to use the tools of our trade to poke, prod, and invade the psychic bodies and minds of entities.
4. We employ the tools of the open-minded skeptic, drawing on past experience and the evidence at hand, while remaining open to new data as it is gathered.
5. At the start of an investigation, we treat entities with respect and we request the same of them.
6. We do not assume that every entity that is unkind, mischievous, or non-communicative is a demon.
7. Under no circumstances do we yell at or threaten entities.
8. In a case where entities are overstepping their bounds, we talk to them—as
you would a partner, neighbor, or coworker—explaining our position and asking them to work with us.
9. We do not believe it is our right to force entities out of a space without first doing a thorough investigation and giving them an opportunity to communicate and be heard.
10. We do not do or distort this work for attention, financial gain, or to seek power over any entity. We undertake this work with Humility, Harmony, and Love.

Tonya Madia, RYT, RMT, LMT, is an author, Reiki Master, medium, yoga teacher, massage therapist, and certified hypnotist (with a focus on past life regression) who believes in the importance of cultivating and trusting your intuition. She has seen firsthand how practices such as yoga, meditation, and Reiki lead to a deeper awareness and understanding of the natural intuitive abilities that we all possess, and for the past decade she has been teaching others how to develop these life-enhancing skills. Her lifelong experiences with the paranormal and encounters as a medium have led her to state with surety that consciousness can survive the death of the physical body. She is frequently invited to investigate everything from private residences and cemeteries to retail stores and community centers and feels blessed to be called on so often to help others on their life journey.

Joey Madia, when he is not investigating or writing about strange phenomena, is a screenwriter, playwright, novelist, actor, director, and Escape room designer. He specializes in bringing true stories to the stage, page, and screen. His screenplay *The Man at the Foot of the Bed* (a paranormal thriller based on a true story) has been a two-time Official Selection and a Beverly Hills Film Festival invitee. His novel series, *The Stanton Chronicles*, combines history, mystery, and the paranormal. He applies the skills of a story analyst and training in a variety of spiritual systems to his paranormal investigations.

Other Books by Tonya and Joey Madia

Living the Intuitive Life: Cultivating Extraordinary Awareness

Watch Out for the Hallway: Our Two-Year Investigation of the Most Haunted Library in North Carolina

Available at Visionary Living Publishing and Amazon (paperback and e-book).

Outer Realms Bath Works

    Specializing in bath and home goods with a paranormal theme. All items are handmade and with materials sourced from the USA.
    We also offer Paranormal Investigator Kits based on our years of experience as field investigators.
    We recently launched a line of creepy dolls and paranormal-themed sock monkeys called Outer Realms Oddities.
    For more information and to place your orders, visit outerrealmsbathworks.com and follow Outer Realms Bath Works on Facebook and Instagram and Outer Realms Oddities on Instagram.

www.ingramcontent.com/pod-product-compliance
Lightning Source LLC
Chambersburg PA
CBHW030854170426
43193CB00009BA/603